Genevieve Stebbins, François Delsarte

Delsarte System of Expression

Genevieve Stebbins, François Delsarte

Delsarte System of Expression

ISBN/EAN: 9783741118456

Manufactured in Europe, USA, Canada, Australia, Japa

Cover: Foto ©Andreas Hilbeck / pixelio.de

Manufactured and distributed by brebook publishing software (www.brebook.com)

Genevieve Stebbins, François Delsarte

Delsarte System of Expression

DELSARTE

SYSTEM OF

EXPRESSION

—— BY ——

GENEVIEVE STEBBINS

WITH THE

ADDRESS OF FRANÇOIS DELSARTE BEFORE THE
PHILOTECHNIC SOCIETY OF PARIS

TRANSLATED FROM UNPUBLISHED MANUSCRIPTS

SECOND EDITION

NEW YORK
48 UNIVERSITY PLACE
EDGAR S. WERNER
1887

CONTENTS.

	PAGE.
Introduction	3

LESSON I.
Decomposing Exercises 11
    Æsthetic Talk.

LESSON II.
Harmonic Poise of Bearing 17
    Æsthetic Talk.

LESSON III.
Principle of Trinity 31
    Æsthetic Talk.

LESSON IV.
The Legs 57
    Æsthetic Talk.

LESSON V.
The Walk 73
    Æsthetic Talk.

LESSON VI.
The Hand 89

LESSON VII.
The Hand.—Continued 99

LESSON VIII.
The Hand.—Continued 103

LESSON IX.
The Arm 107

LESSON X.
The Arm.—Continued 111

Contents.

LESSON XI.
The Arm.—Continued 115

LESSON XII.
The Torso 121

LESSON XIII.
The Head 129

LESSON XIV.
The Head.—Continued 137

LESSON XV.
Active Agents of the Eye 143

LESSON XVI.
Profiles 155

LESSON XVII.
The Lips and the Jaw 161

LESSON XVIII.
Grammar of Pantomime 167

LESSON XIX.
A Gamut of Expression in Pantomime 177

LESSON XX.
The Voice 187

LESSON XXI.
Color 219

Order of Exercises for Systematic Practice 234

Index 257

ÆSTHETIC GYMNASTICS.

		PAGE
1.	Decomposing Exercises: Fingers, Hand, Forearm, Entire arm, Head, Torso, Foot, Lower leg, Entire leg, Entire body, Eyelids, Lower jaw,	12
2.	Harmonic Poise of Bearing: Standing, Change of centre of gravity forward, back and sideways, Rotation, Poise when seated	18
3.	Gestures from the significant zones, mental, moral and vital	49
4.	Standing in significant attitudes	66
5.	The walk	73
6.	Stage falls: Back fall, Front fall, Kneeling, Bowing, Sitting, Rising from sitting, Rising from back fall, Rising from front fall, Rising from kneeling, Pivoting, Rising on toes	83
7.	Sinking wrist, Serpentine movement, Feather movement	95
8.	Opposition of torso and arms, Gladiator oppositions	101
9.	The command "Go," Evolution of motion in arms, Involution of motion from action to repose, Involution of body, Evolution of body,	104
10.	Spiral movement	108
11.	Spiral movement followed by extension of arms in breadths	113

		PAGE
12.	Primary oppositions of head and arm: Mental or normal calm of being, Resigned appeal to heaven, Accusation, Imprecation, Remorse, Deep thought, grief or shame, Reproach, Repulsion from affection, Pathetic protest or benediction.....................	117
13.	Direct, circular and oblique movements for right arm and hand............................	124
14.	Rotation of head in various attitudes.........	134
15.	Lid exercises...............................	140
16.	Brow exercises	151
17.	Nostril exercise...........................	158
18.	Mouth exercise...........................	163
19.	Gamut of expression in pantomime...........	177

    Scene I. You are standing idly in a room: a step on the stairs attracts your attention. The door opens to admit a person for whom you have an affection. You greet this person in delighted surprise.

    Scene II. Receiving no response from the object of your greeting, you increase the courtesy of your salutation, with repeated assurances of your affection.

    Scene III. Your greeting increases in ardor. Receiving no response, you express surprise and affectionate protest.

    Scene IV. The object still shows great doubt of your love; and, consequently, you intensify your expressions of devotion.

    Scene V. No effect is produced on object. In great surprise you ask the reason: "Does he think you guilty of some wrong to him?" You attest your innocence with great vehemence.

ÆSTHETIC GYMNASTICS.   vii

Scene VI. Continued disbelief in your truth and innocence enrages you. You make, however, one final effort for self-control, but show extreme anger in bearing and face.

Scene VII. Your passion has now passed beyond your control, and you order the object of it to leave your presence.

Scene VIII. While gazing in anger at object, as in final attitude of Pantomime 7, its aspect changes into something which paralyzes you with terror, appalls you and fills you with loathing.

Scene IX. You glance toward object. To your amazement, another transformation has taken place. A vision of beauty is before you. Great astonishment depicted on face. You are attracted toward vision. It recedes. You beseech it to remain with you, but it vanishes, leaving you prostrate.

LIST OF CHARTS, ILLUSTRATIONS, ETC.

	PAGE.
Chart I. Criterion	39
II. Attitudes of the legs	72
III. Conditional attitudes of the hand	97
IV. Circle	125
V. Zones of the head	131
VI. Attitudes of the head	135
VII. Divisions of the head	136
VIII. Attitudes of the eyeball	142
IX. The brow	143
X, XI. Combinations of brow and upper lid	152, 153
XII. Expressions of the eyebrow	154
Profile cuts	155
XIII. Expressions of the nose	159
XIV. Expressions of the mouth	164
XV. Vowels	199
XVI. Consonants	200
XVII. Symbolic colors	226

ADDRESS

— OF —

FRANÇOIS DELSARTE

— BEFORE THE —

PHILOTECHNIC SOCIETY OF PARIS.

(Translated from unpublished manuscripts.)

GENTLEMEN: There reigns without doubt in the bosoms of this assembly an opinion entirely incorrect upon the nature and the end of those things that you expect to hear to-day. Now, I cannot lend myself to a deception; and I wish, to commence with, to disabuse your minds of error. I am told that a number of persons present, founding their suppositions upon a precedent recently established in this society, are persuaded that they are going to hear me recite or sing. It will not be so, gentlemen. I shall neither sing nor recite, because I care less to show you what I can do than to tell you what I know.

I am simply going to discuss before you a question of art, that is all; and I have not even the power to offer you a prepared discourse. My memory, singularly rebellious, will not respond to the exigencies of a predetermined text. However, notwithstanding this infirmity, notwithstanding the weakness and inevitable incorrectness of the form, I come to you with the same confidence that I feel in the midst of my pupils. This confidence, gentlemen, has, I think, a triple reason of being. Primarily, the justice of your mind, which, I am sure, will not throw away a savory fruit, because of the coarseness of its envelope. Then the novelty, the absolute novelty of the things I have to teach you; and, finally, the profit that your heart, to which I intend above all to address myself, will gain.

Let me then speak to you, in all frankness, of the art that I study with love and in the exercise of which I have grown old. That established, I come to what is, gentlemen, the object of this lecture. The question is of art; of art disengaged from its applications; of art in itself; of art of which the beginning and the end are in God, and of which the genesis upon this earth remounts to the cradle of creation. This point of departure, gentlemen, is high without doubt; and, at the side of the engagement I have taken, does it not constitute to your eyes a strange contrast? What, formulate here the express promise of a new theory on the subject of a question declared old as the world! It is because art, notwithstanding the antiquity of its origin, is still, from a didactical point of view, unknown even to those who profess it. It is because no one has ever known how to disengage the principles which constitute it from its applications; and so it has never once been defined.

I do not exaggerate, gentlemen; and, however extreme may seem to you the terms of this declaration, I have not in announcing them said one word too much. You will soon recognize this. Yes, the essential and subjective nature of art, its constitutive and organic form, its cause, its beginning and its end; the constitution of its powers, their genesis or their modes of evolution and transformation, their interior organism, their reason of being and their special object; the sort of activity they affect in view of that object; the hierarchic order which rules their harmony, that is to say, the law in virtue of which is produced their successive predominance or their equality of equilibrium—all of this seems to have never been made the subject of a single remark, and the most profound ignorance still reigns upon these initial questions—upon these questions, outside of which æsthetics does not exist. It is because, gentlemen, that even as God, art hides itself in light! It is because that there it rests, as inaccessible to vain curiosity as to egotistic speculation. It is because its transparent beauties cannot be contemplated except by that clearness of vision which belongs only to the pure in heart.

You will soon understand me. You are, gentlemen, more or less touched by a work of art. Very well. When this work moves and charms you, do you know what it is you admire in it, and upon what condition you admire it? You admire it, gentlemen, when you re-find yourselves in it; and if you applaud, it is only on the condition of your recognizing in it something of your own character. It is because it affects, at least partly, your ways, your temperament; it is because it enters into your habits; it is because it flatters and caresses, in descending to your level, your tastes or your crazes. In one word, you love it as you love a mirror. But let a work of art be elevated never so little above the level that surrounds you, let it deviate never so little from the habitual current of this level, let it ruffle your prejudices, or cross your passions, cease to flatter your personality,—finally, let the stamp of your individuality seem to be effaced, then you cease to comprehend it, or rather you do not wish to comprehend, and however superior this work may be, nay, even because of this superiority, no longer being within your range, it has lost all title to your admiration in losing all that charmed you in it.

Thus, let a symphony of Beethoven or Mozart be announced, and crowds will rush to hear it, and with what transports of admiration will they not applaud! While, strange contrast, gentlemen, the torrents of harmony that God has poured into us, the marvelous concerts which He there directs, as it were, in person, find no listeners, and these ravishing spectacles, these ineffable and mysterious representations which are produced in the centre of our beings, in the transluminous obscurities of our souls—representations to which the divine goodness invites us every hour, and which costs not even the pain of a displacement,—all that cannot conquer our indifference, or rather our repulsion, and it is in the solitude, which we disdainfully abandon, that the supreme artist works and produces his most adorable masterpieces.

Why is this so, gentlemen, why? Ah, always for the same cause. It is that man is a voluntary spectator only of his own works. It is that he esteems and admires only himself. It is that he searches in everything himself—it is, again I say it, that he loves only himself, and all that is not that self annoys and wounds him. One of two things is necessary in art: either that the divine work proposed to be contemplated shall be abased to the level of man; or that he elevates himself to its height. Now, man raises himself with difficulty, and through a lamentable tendency, fruit of his fall, he fatally yields to the laws of gravity. Thus, as long as the work of God has not been by man, under pretext of progress, altered, disfigured, coarsened, he passes before it a cold and indifferent spectator and disdainfully turns away his head.

It is there that we must seek the cause of so many accredited errors, of so many dangerous Eutopias, and, in particular, of that profound ignorance that I have just signalized. However, let us hasten to recognize that this deplorable tendency, which makes us fly from the light when darkness seems more favorable to our dreams, is not entirely unconquerable. Simplicity of heart and right willing can do much. Now, the attention you are kindly giving me seems to testify to your good will; so, counting on that disposition, I desire to show to you the marvels that God works in each one of us, and, if enough time is accorded me, to give you some feeble idea of them. I do not despair of making you admire them; and, in raising you to the source of all art, love their author.

But, before all, some general considerations seem to me necessary. First, a word upon the moral action of art ; then, we will prove by undeniable reasons the permanent shallowness of its teachings; and, finally, we will deduce from its interior organism the statement of its powers, of their procession, of their special mode of activity, of their reason of being, and of their particular object. We will deduce from these grave and luminous questions the didactic basis of serious æsthetics; for I do not call æsthetic those commonplaces and those puerilities that form the entire basis of those so-called lessons that are ambitiously published under that title—Art ! Let us contemplate together this sovereign power which conquers all hearts in moving the sentiments; power which calms our sorrows and doubles our pleasures; power irresistibly sympathetic, of which the magic sceptre extends not only over heart and brain, but over all nature. It is by means of it that the artist transforms and animates inorganic bodies, in stamping upon them the character of his life, his soul and his mind; and by it that, pilgrim upon this earth, he yet leaves here imperishable traces of his being. It is, indeed, always by the subjective virtues of this ineffable power that he fixes fugitive things, gives permanence to what is momentary and actuality to that which is no more. Thus he himself lives on in what by itself has no life.

Ah, gentlemen, there are no joys more durable, more noble, or more holy, than those which are drawn from the sources of art. It is because these pure sources do not borrow from earth the virtues they communicate. One feels in their presence a consoling charm, a serenity of soul, and beatific burnings that are not of this world, where all joy is as ephemeral as it is vain. In order to convince ourselves, let us throw a glance around us. What find we? No pleasure which is not followed by deception or satiety; no joy which does not bring some trouble; no affection which does not hide a bitterness, a sorrow, or even a remorse! The sad certainty of being soon and forever separated from all that is dear to us, I ask you, gentlemen, I ask you, would not the thought of this dreadful perspective, where the soul touches already the horror of solitude, be sufficient to poison the few joys offered to our short existence? But where are these considerations leading me, and have I not the air, gentlemen of preaching you a sermon? Such, however, is not my design; and if this form wounds you, accuse only the subject which occupies me; for art and prayer so confound themselves in one ineffable unity that I cannot separate the two things. [Applause.]

Since you encourage me, I will proceed. All is, then, more or less deceiving for man in this world. All about him changes and passes away; all he thinks to possess he sees vanish in his hand. He does not even possess himself. His body wears out, grows old. He assists, day by day, and without being able to remedy it, at his own disorganization. All betrays him; his senses even; his senses so intimately united to his being; his senses, whose appetites he has so often caressed, and to which he has sacrificed so much, like unfaithful servants, they, too, betray him in their turn. And, at last, the elements which constitute this poor body enter some day into open revolt and tend to fly, as if in horror, from each other. But under the ashes of this body, under these ruins which are animated still by a portion of life, dwells a soul, young, always young (for it is immortal), whose perpetual youth brings it torture. For this soul loves, loves notwithstanding the deceptions of its hard experiences. It loves because it is young; loves because, finally, it is *soul* and its condition of being is loving. But if it loves, it wishes to be loved in return; and here begins its agony. For under the hideousness of this body which disfigures and dishonors, it feels forever separated from what it calls its happiness, that happiness toward which, in despite of its ardent desires, it dares not henceforward throw even a furtive glance, feeling as if degraded under the ignominy of its vestment of rags.

Picture to yourselves, gentlemen, a beautiful young girl, to whom a voice of authority says with bitter and inflexible accent: "You are young, you are beautiful, you love your affianced more than yourself, you enjoy this youth which renders you seductive to his eyes, you are happy and proud of that beauty which has conquered his heart. Well, all this shall vanish. This body, magnificent veil thrown over your soul, and of which the transparence to-day charms the eye, to-morrow shall bear the stigmata of a premature old age, and henceforward you will appear no longer to your well-beloved but under this repelling mask!" What would become, I ask you, what would become of the poor child? Would she dare, could she, thus disfigured, offer herself to the view of him who until then seemed to have eyes only for her?

Such is the soul, gentlemen, such is the soul, buried under the ruins of the body. Well, for this poor soul, solitary and desolate, there are still joys, ineradicable joys, which, as we have already said, cannot be measured with those which the world can offer. These joys,—it is art which gives them, art raised upon the wings of faith. Ah, gentlemen, one is never too old to taste those joys. One does not age in the spheres of art. Still better, the more that man feels himself weighed down by years, the more his deceptions have been numerous, the more he has been deceived, deserted, maltreated by fortune, the more the trials of life have been multiplied and severe, the more apt he is to receive the delectations of which art is the imperishable source.

But whence comes this vivifying fecundity of art? Whence comes the sovereign and irresistible dominion which it exercises over all hearts? From its celestial origin. Yes, gentlemen, from its celestial origin. Art is divine in its principles, divine in its essence, divine in its action, divine in its end. And what is, in effect, the essential principles of art? Are they not, taking them together, the Good, the True, and the Beautiful? And their action, and their end, —are they other than a tendency incessantly directed toward the realization of these three terms? Now the Good, the True, and the Beautiful can be found only in God. Thus, art is divine in the sense that it emanates from His divine perfections; in the sense that it constitutes for us even the idea of those perfections; and, above all, in the sense that it tends to realize in us, about us, and beyond us this triple perfection that it draws from God.

Art is, then, definitively, a mysterious agent, of which the sublime virtues work in us, by contemplative paths, the subjection of divine things. The Beautiful is not usual in this world. To convince ourselves we have only to throw around a rapid glance. Nothing that presents itself to our view realizes the Beautiful of which we have an intuition. We ourselves, gentlemen, whatever may be the complaisance with which we proclaim ourselves the masterpieces of creation, and however well founded may be this opinion, let us not deceive ourselves; we are not beautiful. Frankly, we are not beautiful! And if I did not fear offending these ladies who are listening to me with such good-natured interest, I would dare to tell to you more exactly my thoughts upon the sad reality of our ugliness, without speaking of the infirmities that we so carefully conceal. Truly, if the artist did not place himself above this reality, more or less deformed; if he could see nothing better made than himself; and if placed face to face with himself he did not soon feel a profound sentiment of pity, acknowledge, gentlemen, that he would be incapable of raising himself to any very elevated height. Thus, for the true artist it is art and not man that he offers to the admiration of man. It is not here the question, as you can well see, of art as conceived by an obscure executor, or such as an eclecticism, more or less confused, teaches in our schools. Neither, and for much stronger reasons, is it a question of that dried-up art mummified by I do not know what naturalism or theoretic synchronism, call it by what name you will, for it is difficult to characterize it. No, it is not a question here of that art,—atheism disguised under the precious title of a new science and which they pretend, to-day, constitutes the basis of æsthetics.

What, art, that emanation from heaven, that vivid radiance of divine virtue shall be thus resigned, as a vile prey into the hands of skepticism, and shall be nothing henceforward but the favorite theme of a sophist, or the pretext for the subtleties of his atheistic preachings! Ah, this cold and negative conception, which carries in its bosom an odor of the sepulchre, could not have come from the brain of an artist. Whosoever has been guilty of this, shows his own ignorance, and, on my faith, knows not the first word of art. Savants who are only savants, have been able to deny God. That can be conceived of, for when the heart does not communicate to the brain its generous burnings which illumine and fecundate; when it does not inflame those intuitions which constitute genius, the mind cannot go very far.

From that comes this cold reasoning condemned to a profound sterility; from that, this dryness of perception and this narrow vision, which explains in some sort the atheism which certain savants profess. Philosophers, also, have denied God. The pride and the blindness into which these latter so easily fall explain their atheism. But for any artist to deny God, God the cause, the beginning and the end of his art, God the source of his inspirations and his genius,—let us say it, gentlemen, without **fear of contradiction, let us proclaim it to the eternal**

honor of art, never has such a monstrosity been
produced, no, never! Never has an artist denied
his God. For him, art is a magnificent objective,
upon whose field appears an entire transluminous
world, and to whose visions he incessantly tends to
unite himself. For him, art is still a mystic fountain
from which escapes a celestial perfume and across
which he feels, he sees, he touches in some sort that
God who fills him with irrepressible raptures.

Now, gentlemen, the type of art of which I am
speaking draws its existence from light and love.
It purifies the life, illumines the mind, makes perfect and sanctifies the soul; then it embraces, con-
sumes and transfigures it to identity with things
divine. Such is the art I honor; such is the art
which consoles one in growing old, and which, in
my life of trials, has made me more than once bless
my sufferings! Such is the art to which I owe the
inestimable happiness of faith; and, finally, gentlemen, such is the art which I contemplate with love,
which I serve with pride, and which I make my
glory everywhere to profess and defend.

Do not misunderstand, I pray you, the sense of my
words. A misunderstanding here would give birth
in your minds to ideas entirely contrary to those
which you ought to deduce from the thesis I defend.
Art in itself, observe, is not what you should love in
art. I will explain: Nothing is aim, nothing is end
upon this earth; all here is transitory; all here is
but a means. Now, art, however elevated in origin

and magnificent in itself, does not constitute an end.
It is and ought to be in our eyes but a means, a
sublime means without doubt, but only a means,
nothing but a means. Any other manner of re-
garding art debases and degrades it, for it is in the
Object and not in the powers that one must seek
the secret of its grandeur. The powers of art are
the wings of the soul. These wings have been
given to indirectly promote its divine ascension!
Now, the soul which stops to contemplate its wings
will never rise; the beauty of the means can thus
make it forget its aim and plunge it into a sensuous
and sad idolatry.

Thus, gentlemen, to respond worthily to the object
of art let us elevate our minds and our hearts until
we reach the contemplation of its sovereign principle;
that is to say, to the source itself of the Beautiful,
the True, and the Good. Thus, thus, *sursum corda!*
Such is for art the Alpha and the Omega, *sursum
corda!!*

After a profession of faith so simple and so exact,
you understand, gentlemen, that it would be difficult
for me to admit, and above all to partake of, the
sensitiveness which certain artists affect for their art.
They love, they say, with sweet complaisance, art
for art. Love art for art! What does that mean?
First of all, it is idolatry; and then this formula, in
those who use it in good faith, testifies to a very
strange error in reflection. It is unintelligent, but it
is not at the same time unintelligible. To love art

for art, is, in plain language, to prefer the work to its object; it is to turn art from its end to the profit of the artist. This last, however, from a certain point of view, cannot well be entirely unintelligent; but, in any case, it does not answer the object of art. What is it that is loved in a symbol? It is the idea, or the thing that it represents, and assuredly not the matter, however skilfully portrayed one supposes it. In the portrait of a friend do we love anything besides the friend? And do we say, in order to render the impression that the resemblance awakens in us, "I love this image for the *image?*" A declaration like that would be, perhaps, flattering for the painter, but I doubt if it would be as much so for the original.

Let us add a last reflection.

If you own one of those costly instruments that are called telescopes, what, may I ask, interests you in it? Why do you value it? Is it not because of the property it possesses of showing to your surprised eyes vast and profound perspectives, invisible without its aid? It is, then, the astounding views brought within the range of your vision that you love the instrument for, and certainly you would not dare to say that you loved the telescope for the telescope. Now, art is the telescope of a supernatural world. In art one must love something besides art if one would know how to love art.

If I have felt obliged to treat with a certain deference the lovers of art for art's sake, ought I to do the same in regard to that crowd of artists who, seeing nothing in their art but an object of fashion, a theme submitted to the caprices of fantasy, make it either the instrument of their vanity or a pretext for a *tour de force?* And what shall I think of those wretched beings who, profaners of the title they bear, incessantly soil art by the base employment of their talent! Ah, gentlemen, do not ask me to express here how revolting to my artistic sentiments and conscience are these lamentable examples. Instead, I should like to recall to you the words of Father Martini in regard to the singers of his day (what would he say of the singers of to-day, if, in punishment for his sins, he were compelled to hear them!). This judicious man observes: "There are voices against which no complaint can be made, but my heart reproaches them, for they can say nothing to it. You pay a singer to move you, and a tight-rope dancer to astonish you, but now it is the singers who are the tight-rope dancers."

Let us pass now to the didactical exposition of art. You are going to hear successively the essential formulas of a technology henceforward fixed upon a solid basis; for it is not a question here of giving free play to the fantasies of the imagination. Far from that. I am going to give a long series of new ideas which will be found strange—without doubt because they are strange to them—by those who compose the pedagogic babel of our schools. But, nevertheless, you will find in them nothing conjectural, nothing hazarded, nothing which does not conform to the severest logic. In this exposition, notwithstanding the novelty of the theories, I wish to bring the exactness and precision of figures. But, you are going to say to me, your premise has not been accepted by us; the accusation of ignorance with which you weigh down an entire corps of teachers rests entirely upon mystic and insufficient proofs. In order to sustain such sweeping assertions you must have something more than theory, more than reasons,—you must give us facts, self-evident facts. Formulate other arguments and prove to us, finally, what you have advanced with so much assurance. So be it. We will leave, then, for awhile, the question of principles, leave transcendental views, and examine facts.

I have affirmed that the initial questions of art are absolutely unknown even to professional artists. I have said that outside of these necessary solutions there is no possible æsthetics. And, finally, I have stated the radical absence of all didactics in official instruction,—instruction which, in general, does not even raise itself to the height of empiricism. I now add, to complete my thought and render it more salient, that nothing defined exists in our schools; there is no regular instruction, no code, no law; and, consequently, no sanction, no possible guarantee against the wanderings and fantasies of each individual master, nothing absolute, nothing which constitutes the character of an organized instruction. **The instruction, as it is at present, is nothing but a** confused mass of recipes, of contradictory precedents and examples, an inextricable chaos of imposed prescriptions without plausible explanations, a labyrinth without issue, where masters and pupils wander only to stay forever buried. You see, gentlemen, instead of subtracting I have added a new cipher to my accusations.

I will not return to the causes of this deplorable absence of principles in men endowed with indisputable talent. I have abundantly indicated them to every mind that from a consequence can draw a principle; and now I am going to prove my assertions by facts, facts which the most skeptical cannot doubt; and as there are some who will believe themselves forced to refute them, I wish to give them the weight of a crushing evidence. I will enter at once the heart of the difficulty, and attack in front the culminating point of the question. It is clear that there exists certain fundamental principles which we have the right to demand from those who proclaim themselves masters and who pretend to teach art. Now, these principles, indispensable laws of all serious instruction, are not, in reality, known, and, consequently, are taught by no one.

I shall also prove to you that neither the school of *Beaux Arts*, nor special schools, nor private masters, suspect even the existence of these principles. I think that my thesis will have been fully shown, and that is what I hope to establish. And, first, as to what concerns the school of *Beaux Arts*.

I seem to hear you offer, as a peremptory argument, the notoriety of the talent and the incontestable merit of the members of that grand institution, the reputation and the éclat of those brilliant individualities of whom the pupils, and with reason, do not even pronounce the name but with legitimate respect. Very well, gentlemen, notwithstanding that illustrious body, the school of *Beaux Arts*, that palladium of æsthetic science, is, as I said at first, the name of a thing which does not exist and never has existed. I see under this title an academic assemblage of specialists, whose individual merit I am far from denying. But these specialists, have they between them a determined scientific basis? What is their systematic entity and their community of belief? Where is their code and, consequently, the possibility of exercising the smallest jurisdiction? Their official reunion, has it ever produced anything which justified the title of school with which they ornament themselves? What is a school that has no settled principles, no established doctrine, no definite instruction? What kind of a school is it whose contradictory methods incessantly let art fall into the domain of fashion, thus subordinating its noble powers to the vagabondage of the senses as well as to the silly variations of caprice and fantasy? Finally, what is a school which, owing to the complete absence of determined rules, surrenders, without defense, to the interior tyranny of an unbridled imagination and to the still more humiliating tyranny of prejudices and tastes, sometimes very abject, of a public to which she submits as a slave when she ought to command as a queen?

This, however, is the negative condition of that which we name the school of *Beaux Arts*. For me, gentlemen, this heterogeneous assembly does not offer, I avow, the grave character of a school. Yes, even though she enclosed in her bosom all the scientific light of the world, the powerlessness and the sterility with which she is struck because of her constitution would authorize me still to say of the school of *Beaux Arts*, there is nothing but the name.

You say: "They teach, however, painting, sculpture, architecture." I do not contradict you; add to the list music, belles lettres, etc. I grant that one can learn there all of those things; but you will not learn art. They form there, if you will have it so, painters, sculptors, musicians; but they form no artists. I would say of science what I say of art, if my subject permitted me. I see men who treat of all sciences except *the science*. I see mathematicians, anatomists, chemists, physicians, etc., but I see no savant.

Let us return to the school of *Beaux Arts*, to what one ought to find there but finds not, as I expect to show by the following argument: Music, eloquence and plastic art are the attributive specialties of an *all* which is taught nowhere and which has not even been defined. Now, the law which governs and binds together these specialties, which shows their original community and their consubstantiality in the triple essence, which contains and rules them as so many agents of which the condition of being is unity; the science which gives the reason of their successive predominance, or of their equilibrium; finally, that unity of principles without which there is no school of art possible,—where is this taught ? Nowhere. Where is this practiced ? Nowhere. Where is this formulated ? Nowhere. Then art-instruction does not exist. Then that which is given the name of instruction in the matter of art proceeds only from an instinct badly defined and arbitrarily interpreted. Then that which one would be able to found and call a school of art cannot be met even in an embryonic state. Then the plan of a school desirable for so many reasons, is still to be conceived,—then, then, all is yet to be found, all is yet to be made, and in regard to all art, every attempt at a constitution will be, even in its root, struck with paralysis, until music, eloquence and plastic art, these three co-necessary bases of art, are taught unitedly as they are together united to the constituent essences of our being. All of this, gentlemen, is absolutely undeniable, and is worth, without doubt, the trouble of a thorough examination.

"But," you still say, "granting that art is not taught as you understand it, you must acknowledge that each of the special branches, of which you would make an indivisible whole, is taught with a certain superiority." Gentlemen, to this I oppose a simple reasoning upon the bearing of which I will not here stop to insist. It is that the part of a whole cannot be seriously appreciated by anyone ignorant of the constitution of this same whole.

Now, to confirm my thesis, let us come to examples; from the academic heights where we have placed ourselves, let us descend to special schools. Let us stop, in order not to make this discourse interminable, at the lessons of the Conservatory, at the same time stating that the abuses found there are not confined to that school, but are reproduced in the actual instruction of all kinds of art.

What passes, then, in the Conservatory? In that school there reign, without control as without contest, arbitrariness and contradiction; there, one finds that the antagonism of masters, each one convinced of his own omnipotent infallibility, because he draws only from himself, and his judgments are without appeal, creates an anarchy, the excesses of which they do not even dream of repressing. There, in effect, all the law rests upon the opinion of the master; all the science dwells in a confused mass of prescriptions and examples that no principle comes to support. Fantasy imposes them, ignorance conforms to them; and the pupils, condemned to mechanically reproduce them, are hardly anything else at the end of their course than the servile copyists of a master without doctrine. No judicious mind will accuse me of characterizing with too much stress such sterile instruction. Slavery is at the root of it; and this slavery opposes the greatest obstacle to that elevation of character and idea, which should belong to the artist. This blind reproduction, which collects the knowledge of men living in frozen art-zones, paralyses and dries up all which nature and a vocation have given to the artist of instinct, of intelligence, and of heart.

I should have very curious revelations to make to you upon this subject which would greatly divert you, if I should read the monumental stupidities which swarm in these undigested collections, published under the title of methods; methods officially approved by the Institute, adopted and consecrated only, here below, to conspire against our happiness, by the Conservatory. But time presses, and I do not wish to give anything that the necessity of my position does not prescribe. Listen, I pray you, to a little anecdote, chosen from among thousands. It is very instructive, and as it is a personal experience, I am able to guarantee its perfect authenticity:

At the age of fourteen, I possessed a tenor voice, to the charms of which I already owed a remarkable success; for, at the side of the grand opera airs which are sung in drawing-rooms, I was applauded for singing the simple lessons of Rudolf. This fact, without precedent, proves clearly enough all that was to be hoped from my future. Thus, notwithstanding my very young age, notwithstanding the formal rules, my admission to the Conservatory was not even opposed. Alas! I had been there hardly six months when, under the killing influence of an unintelligent instruction, I saw this voice, upon which I had built such glowing hopes, disappear! Is not this the story of so many unfortunate young men who are seemingly condemned by the nature even of their studies, to incessantly destroy the precious gifts upon which depends sometimes their entire existence? I had, then, already lost my voice, thanks to the cares of the Conservatory; but, however unfortunate that was, that loss did not make me entirely abandon the hope of being something some day. Courage came back to me, little by little, for I expected from art that which instinct could no longer give me. " Nature can do nothing more for me," I said, "so why brood over it? Tears will not give back to me the voice I have lost." So, taking heart, I added: "Who knows but that some day I shall be grateful for this loss, which now fills me with desolation? Who knows if this misfortune does not conceal a benefit of Providence? I have now no longer the right to be a mediocre artist. The study of science, the study of art above all, offers, without doubt, powerful resources. And then, the possession of this good, which does not perish, is it not a thousand times preferable to the natural qualities that one is always on guard against losing?"

Thus I consoled myself and prepared to follow, with all the strength of my being, the conquest of the science which was to make of me a great artist.

And this deception was more cruelly felt than the
first! I had had successively the best masters of
the Conservatory, and that during four years, without being able to get the first notion of that science
from which I expected my salvation; for there, no
theory supported the execution. Thus, that which
was imposed upon me by one teacher as absolutely
necessary, was unpityingly interdicted by the others
as ridiculous or injurious, without either the one or
the other deigning to support their dictum upon the
authority of an established principle. Each one,
from the height of his infallibility, claimed your
attention as the living law, and posed as the type of
the Good, the True and the Beautiful, and you dared
not let a doubt appear, or even hazard a question.
There only remained to the poor student, tormented
by the contradictory prescriptions of his masters, to
make respectfully an act of faith before each individual omniscience. Forced to servilely copy my
masters, I reached the point of being able, as some
acknowledged, to reproduce faithfully enough their
manner.

I was often called upon to recite the same scene
to four masters of declamation, from whom I received alternate lessons. I was forced to render,
turn by turn, this scene according to the dictum of
each one. Now it happened to me sometimes,
either by thoughtlessness or mischief, to represent
to one the manner of the other. I was certain, then,
to be thought detestable, and on that occasion it

was upon my head that rained the numerous blows that these gentlemen did not hesitate to strike at one another. For instance, one day I wished to recite to them these verses of Philomen and Baucis:

> "Neither gold nor grandeur renders us happy;
> Those two divinities accorded to our vows
> Only goods uncertain, but pleasures untranquil."

The first professor to whom I addressed myself, declared that there was but one manner of saying them well, and that one manner, you can easily comprehend, gentlemen, could not fail to be his own.

"You must," said he, "express those lines with amplitude, with dignity, with nobleness." Thereupon, my professor declaimed them in his most sonorous and majestic voice. He raised his eyes to heaven, rounded his gestures, and took a heroic pose.

"You must," said he, interrupting himself, "give to this masterpiece all the importance it deserves. It is by this touching and elevated form of expression that one captivates the public. Ennoble as much as possible your inflections and your gesture. The expression here cannot be too grand. Show yourself, by the elevation of your manner, worthy of the lessons which I give you. Force your voice, give to it all the extent of which it is capable. Good; that is it. And now, enlarge your gesture."

"Ah," said I, "at last I possess the noble manner of rendering these beautiful verses. It is evident that one cannot reasonably give them another meaning." The next day, after having practiced with all my might the noble manner which had been impressed upon me as the only one admissible, I went to my second professor entirely persuaded that he would have only congratulations for me. Ah, yes! I had not finished the second verse when a shrugging of the shoulders, accompanied by a formidable burst of laughter, very humiliating for my noble manner, suddenly closed my mouth.

"Why this emphatic tone, this preaching?" said he. "Where did you pick up this ranting? My friend, you are grotesque. In what parish do you intend to preach this pompous bit? Frankly, your manner of reciting these lines is intolerable. That is not the way, my friend. These lines should be said naturally, simply, and with all possible *bonhommie*. Why, think, it is the good La Fontaine who is speaking, the good La Fontaine (dwelling on each syllable), the good La-Fon-taine; do you understand? Do you comprehend now, how far you were, poor boy, from where you should place yourself in order to conceive the true spirit of that work? For there is only one manner of rendering it faithfully, I mean conforming to the views of the author. Listen, and try to profit from this simple and natural example."

Here the professor caressed his snuff-box, looked fixedly at his audience, pinched his lips and maliciously depressed their corners, slightly contracted his eyes, elevated his brows, shook his head five or six times from right to left, and commenced the lines in a high, concentrated and slightly nasal voice. "Ah," said I, marveling at the intellect that he made shine out in the lines; "there can be no other manner. This is so full of *bonhommie*, simplicity and nature. How far removed from the pompous and declamatory fashion of my first professor. I understand now, how ridiculous must have seemed my first recitation. Bravo, my dear master! It is superb. I shall try to profit by the admirable lesson that I have just received." Lo, behold me again, working on a new basis and saying to myself: "At last I possess the natural manner which becomes the spirit of this charming piece. I wonder what impression it will produce to-morrow upon my third professor."

The moment so much wished for arrived. First of all I take a pose and commence those elliptical expressions which had been indicated to me the evening before. Then I attack my subject in a voice which exactly recalls the master, so much had the example impressed me; and with the confidence which the sentiment of the natural inspires me and with which I was penetrated, hear me saying: "Neither gold, nor grand ——" Ah! like lightning came the brutal interruption, not allowing me even to finish the fourth word.

"Idiot!" cries my third professor, "what do you mean by this old-man manner; why this cracked voice? Why this Cassandra-like tone? From what crow have you learned it? How, stupid, do you dare to come with a work so parodied? You have ruined those beautiful lines, you wretch. All that you did was ignoble!"

"But, sir —"

"Be still and do not dare to answer me, or I'll turn you out of the room. However, I will forgive you this time; but never play the clown here again. Be at least decent in my class, and try and conform to the lessons I give you. You can do very well when you wish, and I am generally pleased with you; but you are, from time to time, subject to certain wanderings of which you must correct yourself. Sometimes you imitate X. You are then detestable, for it is a caricature. It is a vulgar type and very dangerous for you. Why, you looked just like him a moment ago. It was hideous! Listen, now, and do not forget my lesson. There is only one manner of saying this, do you hear? There is but one manner, and this is it."

Hereupon, my professor takes a pensive attitude; then, as if crushed under a sorrowful remembrance, he slowly throws a look around him in which is painted the bitterness of a deep deception. He heaves a sigh, raises his eyes to Heaven, still preserving the inclination of his head, and commences in a deep, veiled tone: "Neither gold, nor grandeur." Here he makes a pause, during which he again lowers his glance and looks about him. He compresses his lips, sorrowfully raises his shoulders, and, slightly extending his arms, continues thus: "renders us happy." Here, again, a pause, during which he lets his arms fall heavily; then he clinches his hands, looks once more to Heaven, but obliquely, this time; lowering the corners of his half-opened mouth, he continues in an imprecating tone: "Those two divinities," here a sigh and distention of members previously contracted, until they relax in complete prostration; "accorded to our vows," etc.

"See," said my master, still filled with the emotion that he had just rendered with an expression at once penetrating and tragic, "see with what art I draw from those lines a pathetic situation. This is what you must imitate. Keep well in mind all you have heard and seen me do. When you are able to extract effects of such high value you can then boast of being able to recite the verse."

"Ah, my dear master, you are right. Yours is the only interpretation worthy of this masterpiece. I am thoroughly convinced, and I will do anything in the world to be able to profit by your magnificent example." Goodness, how beautiful I thought; decidedly neither my *noble* professor nor my *natural* professor understood this piece. The one is pompous; the other vulgar in his efforts to be natural, and neither the one nor the other found the emotional side. Assuredly, I now have the only method of reciting these lines. What a splendid effect I shall produce to-morrow in the class of my fourth professor. What astonishment I shall cause to my comrades when they see what scenic effects I shall draw from the words. They will expect nothing. I can already see their surprise; ah, they will be overwhelmed. I again commenced my studies with incredible ardor, so much so that the next day I felt myself sufficiently ready to produce my effect. Alas! a new deception for me. My fourth master was even more unpitying than the others.

"Why, my poor boy," said he; "where did you get that sepulchral tone? What does this cavernous voice signify here, and why this lugubrious pantomime? Heavens! you are giving me a melodrama, and according to you the piece should be conceived in view of a boulevard of crime. I am sure you have studied in the bottom of a cave. Come, come, my poor boy, you have not done well. I thought you more intelligent. So you cannot understand what you read? I wonder by what strange aberration of mind you have succeeded in thus maiming poor La Fontaine. What has he done to you to be so maltreated?"

Alas, alas! thought I, can it be that my dramatic professor is as absurd as the two others? Truly I find nothing to reply to the criticism of this professor; he is a hundred times right. The method that was prescribed yesterday then seemed to me sublime, while now I clearly see that it is only ridiculous. Can this master tell me the right way?

I will spare you, gentlemen the reasoning of this professor. I could prolong this experience indefinitely, but what end would it serve? A hundred professors would have had the same pretensions, and it is strongly to be suspected that among them I would not have found two of the same opinion. Thus I went from class to class, wearily hearing the conflicting falsities of my ignorant professors. But the truth,—where was it? Between these conflicting renderings, imposed by men of equal merit and equal authority, which was right? From the above experience I naturally drew this conclusion: Since each one in particular says that he alone has the truth, it follows that from their own statements all are false. This is evident and their accord upon that is absolute. In effect, my noble professor, my natural professor, my dramatic professor and my euphonic professor could be equally taxed with absurdity and that by an Areopagus against which there could be no appeal, for there would always be among them three against one. "However," added I, "is it not possible that one among them could sustain himself against his contradictors? Assuredly; but how to choose? I was absolutely ignorant of the means of discerning the true from the false; and this means, initial in matters of art and so desirable in a case like mine, is precisely the means I have never been taught, and of which they have never spoken."

Another supposition came to haunt me. Who knows, notwithstanding their declarations, which a jealous rivalry renders suspicious, who knows but they are all right? For can it be believed that artists whose talent is so much admired are, in that which touches the essence of their art, so equally absurd? This is inadmissible at the tribunal of commonsense. But, on the other hand, is it less inadmissible that methods so dissimilar can have the same claim to our approbation? That would be to land us in chaos. As well declare truth contradictory of itself. Now, I do not feel myself enough of a Hegelian to sustain such an enormity. Between these two abysses rises before me an insolvable dilemma. "If these masters are wrong," said I finally, "one must despair of art; for where can be found to teach it men of more incontestable talent; and if they are right what, then, is truth? It is only an empty word. In one or the other case, I do not see any possible solution."

Judge, gentlemen, of my perplexity between the contradictions, where an arbitrary instruction incessantly plunged me. I confess that under the weight of these continual alternatives, I had lost the sentiment of the true and the false. Art was hardly anything more to my eyes than the servile imitation to which I had been forced. It is thus that is formed, held together and mutually admired, so much lazy, self-sufficient mediocrity. Thus it was that, founded entirely upon the blind reproduction of mute examples, the only point I could draw from my exercises was the talent of execution; and Heaven knows how I had acquired even that, since in the Conservatory all consisted in imitating without comprehending. Nevertheless, they said, I had finished my studies. Then came a cruel awakening and measuring in despair the depth of my ignorance. I sorrowfully cried: "What, then, have I learned." It would take too long, gentlemen, for me to tell you here how I escaped from those paths of slavery. The science which forms the basis of art, that science which it was my dream to possess, was not to be found where I had sought. I had asked for it in vain from my special men, from my masters, their performance or their writings. Nothing, nothing which justified so much lying promise; nothing but phrases as false as they were sonorous; and when I ardently asked for a principle, a law, a reason, my questions were invariably lost in the void.

In face of these nothings, and pushed forward by irresistible aspirations, it was necessary to resign myself to seeking the solution of questions which, once asked, left me neither rest nor peace as long as they remained unsolved. And how was I to obtain that peace? How make descend on me this sudden revelation the power of which was to transfigure my entire being? How and by whom was my intelligence illuminated? Gentlemen, I feel that I owe you this history; but I also feel that strength and time are now lacking me to do the subject ample justice; and though here is the place to tell it to you, I shall have the courage to postpone this recital to a more opportune occasion. I do not wish to, I ought not to, I cannot, disfigure by touching lightly facts of such importance. No, gentlemen, to-day I will not tell you; neither will I say to you how many years of labor, of watchings and of tears the pursuit of these solutions has cost me. God alone knows. But Providence has blest my work, and has not left unfruitful so many and so persevering researches, researches which, certainly, had neither happiness nor success for motive, but to which I was spurred by a profound love of truth, pushed as far as an entire sacrifice of my time, my health and my repose. In the field of investigation one must not count years. Time does not preserve what it has cost us *no* time to create. This truth has every day a new confirmation. Thus, it is not rare to see men consume their lives in sustaining theories more seductive than solid, that a dangerous precipitation has pushed prematurely into the light. The theorist wishes to reap too soon, and so publishes guessed-at propositions, counting, not without some reason, upon the incompetency of the large number of the uneducated many and the laziness and inertia of the special few, in a matter of experimentation.

Henceforth, there is no rectification possible for him. He has advanced and dare not recoil; he must sustain, at all costs, that which he now knows is at bottom unsustainable, for he has built his fame and fortune upon an erroneous theory, and though he comprehends all the evil that he does in propagating error (error of which the consequences are so often lamentable), rather than say "I am wrong," he sacrifices, to prop up this shameful edifice, his time, his repose and even his talent. Thus, more than one life proves barren that a little more patience and maturity would have rendered fruitful.

I have not wished to expose myself to the dangers of such a shipwreck. In the course of my explorations, ten times I have had to retrace my steps and rectify my ways, without its costing a single wound to my self-love; and, God be thanked, have been able to do this in an era when the mania to see one's self in print is pushing so many into an unripe publicity. I pride myself upon having devoted to science and art thirty-five years of research, crowned by important discoveries, without one line from me, with my consent, finding its way to publication.

These, gentlemen, are the reasons upon which I found the hope that my life will not have been useless to science and art. But my time is limited, and carried away by the richness of my subject I have let my improvisations take unexpected proportions, and have only swept the territory and prepared the way for the complete exposition that I had reserved for you. Now, at the moment of commencing the culminating point of my thesis, inexorable time warns me that your sustained and good-natured attention, after having been for so long my amiable listeners, must begin to be worn out. ["Go on, go on," from the audience]

I am happy, gentlemen, to find that you take such an interest in the subject which occupies us; but, whatever may be my desire to satisfy you, the late hour reminds me that there only remains time enough to give in dry and abstract formulas the fundamental principles of art, the development, comprehension and complete demonstration of which I shall, to my great regret, be forced to defer to another conference. The pursuit of the art which I exercise has led me, naturally, into the domain of science; and, thanks to the deductions of a rigorous logic, I have been forced to the conclusion that there is between them identity of scientific methods (and I hold at present their highest generalization). Right or wrong, I look on myself as upon the eve of enriching my country with a series of discoveries of which antique philosophy despaired, and with reason! I am at least certain of having determined the fixed basis of art, realizing, in so doing, that which serious minds had considered as impossible. Thus, gentlemen, and in virtue even of the immutability of the basis of art, æsthetics, lost to-day in the chaos of oratoric fantasies,—æsthetics, henceforward disengaged from all conjecture, will be truly constituted under the severe forms of a positive science. In an abstract, made of the means of execution that the artist ought to learn before treating of any subject, two things are first necessary: (1) Know what he ought to seek in the subject; (2) know where to find what he seeks. He must have, in the first place, the faithful signal of the sought-for thing; in the second, the means of surely finding it.

Now, to know what he ought to seek, the artist needs an exactly-formulated definition of art, of its object, of its aim and of its means. This definition, to be practical, should carry the irrefragible character of a demonstration. Also, to surely find what he seeks he needs an infallible criterion, which should, like an inextinguishable torch, direct its possessor in the vast field of examination. I have said that, first of all, the artist must have a practical definition; that is to say, a formula which bears the character of a demonstration, and which shall be for him the signal of the thing which he seeks and wishes to realize. At the present speaking, nothing which constitutes art has been determined, and there exists for the artist no definition from which he can draw the least profit in view of his work. A simple example will prove this assertion. Let us suppose that I wish to produce a plastic image. I naturally ask myself how I shall arrive at realizing the Beautiful in this work. And, first of all, I wish to remark that it is not the question here of my personal taste. If I had only that to consult I should not be embarrassed. But my personal judgment would have the force of a law only in my own eyes; and, in matters of taste, the Chinese, the Esquimaux and the negro could, with reason, oppose to me their type as the perfect expression of the Beautiful.

Now, the Beautiful, of which I wish to realize the conditions, cannot be subordinated to the variations of taste. It escapes, I feel it, from this sentiment, conceived in the more or less deformed surroundings which a prejudiced education has imposed upon me. The Beautiful is then, or should be, in reason even of its consubstantiality with the True and the Good, entirely disengaged from the capricious influences which attach to taste. In effect, gentlemen, the Beautiful is something sovereign and supernatural, which impresses itself upon our admiration in despite even of our surroundings, because it is in its nature absolute. But what is, definitely, this absolute, unchangeable Beautiful, of which I conceive the existence, but which I cannot explain? Where find it; how obtain it? Finally, how dispose of this sovereign power so as to invariably associate it with my works? Who will tell me?

From all this, one important and well-attested fact, already disengaged itself for me: It is that the search for the Beautiful is not an affair of taste, for the reason that taste is born, developed and purified under the impression of the Beautiful, and does not discern it *a priori*. Thus it cannot be a guide. I have need, you can well comprehend, gentlemen, I have need of specific instruction of a superior order. I need Ariadne's thread to guide my search and fix my choice in this labyrinth of types and forms, which offer themselves to me with equal claims to my preference, and seem equally founded, to determine the absolute Beautiful. I need a luminous formula, a practical definition, which shall carry with it the demonstration which I seek, — a demonstration with the aid of which I shall be able to realize, logically and surely, the Beautiful in each part, in the general attitude of my statue, in the proportions, the delicacy of the plans, the purity and the correctness of the details, which, for instance, the mouth and the nose constitute; for each feature of the face ought, in its turn, to become the object of an especial examination and an especial execution. I have, then, I will suppose, and in order to speak of but one detail among those which ought successively to occupy me in the general plan of my work, — I have, then, to realize, in virtue of a practical definition, the most beautiful nose possible. Now, gentlemen, where find, I ask you, where find a definition, a formula, a teaching which answers, in the most remote way, to this actual and incessant need of the worker, and which directs him, be it never so little, toward the constitution of the Beautiful. Nowhere, gentlemen, absolutely nowhere.

After that, will you suggest to me the magnificent and sonorous definition of Plato? So be it. But how are you going to extract from that definition, or any other of the same character, the plastic condition of a beautiful nose? [Laughter.] Do not laugh, gentlemen; one must specify something. Now tell me, I pray, what profit can the sculptor draw from it for the nose, which actually preöccupies

him and of which he wishes to determine the form?
I can see my sculptor turning and re-turning in his
head the terms of that definition which charmed him
elsewhere, and which he admired *a priori:* "The
Beautiful is the splendor of the True." There is, in
effect, in that definition a character of grandeur
which seizes and subjugates you. But however that
may be, the poor man will not be any the less embarrassed to draw from it his nose. "What form,"
says he to himself, "what proportion and what character shall I give to that nose to bring out the splendor of the True of which Plato speaks?" Frankly,
gentlemen, a similar attempt could never be made
in earnest. One feels immediately that it contains
nothing practical, nothing that can be deduced to
the profit of art.

However, one also feels that the Beautiful does
not proceed from a conventional source; that it is
absolute, unchangeable. Instinct proclaims that;
hence it must be founded upon laws, upon eternal
laws. This is what no one will be able to deny.
But these laws, of which we feel the existence, are
formulated nowhere. "That," you will reply, " has
not prevented the Beautiful from being produced in
many a work of art." Undeceive yourselves, gentlemen, and do not conclude, from its forgetfulness,
from its absence or its ignorance, that a formula
is useless. The artist, deprived of the knowledge
of a criterion which governs his art and to which he
should submit all his work, can never be but the

servile and blind copyist of works produced in a former and more enlightened epoch. The actual state of art proves, in a lamentable manner, that one cannot do without solidly-established principles. Thus the realization of the Beautiful in plastic art, for instance, is no longer with us, but an affair of pure imitation or copy. The conditions of the Beautiful come to us exclusively from antiquity, and it is this far-off epoch, which in this age of progress we hold so cheaply, that to-day still imposes them on us. So true is it that, to attain the Beautiful, one cannot do without a formula; that is to say, a fixed principle. Now, antiquity holds that place and constitutes for us our law. We have nothing, in effect, absolutely nothing but tradition. Everything produced outside of that is miserable; so much so that, from copy to copy, art has degenerated and been lowered, finally, to the piteous state to which we now see it reduced.

Truly, it would be otherwise, and art would not follow that incessantly declining path if the artist, possessor of a law, could realize the Beautiful outside of the traditions which hold him in such absolute slavery. Some have, in these latter days, protested, with apparent reason, against that state of bondage in which art has, for many centuries, existed. Without doubt, a reäction of this kind is part of a good movement; but it is seriously to be feared that it will end but in greater corruption. As for me, I have not a doubt in regard to it. It is necessary, to justify and fructify this movement, to oppose to the antique formula, of which one has no longer the secret, stable principles drawn from the source of an infallible law. One should substitute for the tradition of the ancients a didactic form, and that is what has not been done,—what they have not had the knowledge to do.

Now, the nothingness found in our instruction brings us back, always and fatally, to antiquity, even though the powers unite to raise themselves against the tyranny of its influence. This tyranny, gentlemen, is such, in effect, that one cannot withdraw from its influence with impunity; and, believe me, in the state of ignorance where we are this tyranny is providential, and one should bless it under penalty of soon relapsing into barbarism. And then, let us be just; how much magnificent talent we owe to its influence! How many geniuses have been formed and developed under the inculcation of precepts drawn from the antique; and what can one oppose, I pray you, to the magnificence of that past with which one pretends definitely to break, at the present day ? Nothing, nothing but a hideous realism based upon the most gross naturalism.

Very well, gentlemen, this sovereign law of the plastic Beautiful I will formulate for you in time and place, and that in a way to be able to realize the conditions with mathematical surety. I reserve for the same occasion the definition of the Beautiful, which, besides, would not here be in its place, since it naturally springs from the capital definition which I have yet to give you,—I mean to say, the definition of art. It is by this, gentlemen, that I intend to terminate this talk.

Here is, then, a practical definition of art; but, first, I should give you that of science, since science constitutes the initial basis of art.

Science is the possession of a criterion of examination against which no fact protests. Art is the generalization and application of it.

Now, science elevates man by subjecting to him the things of this world. Art supernaturalizes those things by identifying him with them. Behold you now, gentlemen, in a very few words, possessors of a definition of science, of which all the known sciences are but attributive expressions. I am going now to complete this definition by a problem, upon the solution of which is based science. Here is the problem: Being given an organic or immanent whole, distinguish the constitutive parts of this whole; establish their harmonic consubstantiality; determine their circumincession;—that is to say, the vivifying principle in virtue of which they co-penetrate; characterize their hierarchic order after an invariable type; signal the forces, the powers and the virtues; and, finally, specify their particular object, their end and their means in view of the part they play in a coëfficient activity.

This problem, gentlemen, can only be solved by the possession of the infallible criterion to which I have just made allusion, and which it rests with me to make known. I defer this question, as I have that of the Beautiful with which it is closely connected. That stated, let us define art from a triple point of view, viz.: ontological, moral, and organic.

Art is at once the knowledge, the possession and the free direction of the agents, by virtue of which are revealed life, mind and soul. It is the application, knowingly appropriated, of the sign to the thing, an application of which the triple object is to move, to convince and to persuade. Art is not, as is said, an imitation of nature. It elevates in idealizing her; it is the synthetic rapport of the scattered beauties of nature to a superior and definite type; it is a work of love, where shine the Beautiful, the True and the Good; it is the symbol of the mysterious degrees of our divine ascension, or of the successive degradations of the fallen soul. Art, finally, is the tendency of the fallen soul toward its primitive purity, or its final splendor; in one word, it is the search for the eternal type.

After having thus defined art, let us examine the nature of its object. Man constitutes this object, and from this point he should be especially studied. What, then, is man as the object of art?

Man is a hypostatic trinity, the immanent activities of whom are revealed by means of a triple organic apparatus. Or: Man is a triple hypostasis, in whose service functionate three organic apparatuses, of which the successive or simultaneous play state and manifest the immanent activities of his being. Or, better still. It is by virtue of a triple mode of organic activities that man reveals the immanent powers of his being.

I ought, because of the capital importance of this definition and to render it more comprehensible, present it to you under diverse forms. I wish to produce it again with greater development, so that you will clearly comprehend the value and the sense of the theorem by which I terminate this talk:

Man, made in the image of God, manifestly carries in his inner being as in his body, the august imprint of his triple causality.

Let us prove this truth. Man feels, thinks and loves. Three organic apparatuses are in him, affected to this triple mode of being in order to manifest the special activities. These three apparatuses show, in virtue of the emanating products of their respective agents, three states under the action of which man appears to us, and determine three languages specially allied to the three faculties which govern his being.

Let us make a resumé of these definitions by the following theorem, which should form the basis of our next demonstrations. Every judicious mind will see in it, without doubt, the character of a plan, ripely conceived, of which the developments embrace the highest spheres of art as of science.

Man considered from the point of view of art, presents three orders of essential functions, each one depending upon a proper and determined organic ap paratus. These apparatuses engender three orders of corresponding products. Thus, there results in the phenomena three states, three species of acts, three languages, each one of which should be studied in itself and in its relations of association, of succession and of hierarchy. *These three orders of functions, of apparatuses and of languages constitute the natural division of the phenomena of the human personality and of its triple causality.*

This manner of looking at man shows us the rôle of his two natures in all their manifestations. To each spiritual function responds a function of the body. To each grand function of the body corresponds a spiritual act. Thus we can at the same time study separately that which is of the spirit and that which is of the body; thus from the concurrence of these two powers in the same person, results the intimate fusion of art and science, which, though each one is born of a different source, nevertheless ally, interpenetrate and reciprocally prove each other.

These demonstrations, will be clear and, above all, practical, when the terms of which they are composed shall have been successively examined, and shall have become the object of an especial development.

And now, gentlemen, let me say to you in terminating this long seance, how profoundly I have been touched by your good-natured sympathy and your reiterated applause. This sympathy, which has sustained me in the unforeseen developments into which this improvisation has led me, permit me to retain;

perhaps I shall have need of it another time. As to the applause with which you have made this hall resound, I feel, and I cheerfully declare, that it is due entirely to the grand idea I proclaim. This applause honors, above all, those whose intelligence is right enough to comprehend it, and whose heart is pure enough to love it.

Introduction.

INTRODUCTION.

"Where, where, can I find the Abbé Delaumosne?" I asked of every one I met in Paris when, some months after my arrival, I found myself settled for the year's study of the French drama, for which I had come.

"Who is the Abbé Delaumosne?" asked M. Regnier, ex-president of the government conservatory, to whom I was applying for lessons.

"He is the compiler of Delsarte's system of dramatic art," I replied; "I want very much to see him, but no one can tell me where to find him."

At last a letter from his publisher, to whom I had written, contained the wished-for address, Nanterre, of whose church, St. Genevieve, the abbé was curé. The next morning found me on my way.

"Nanterre!" shouts the guard. I descend and look about me. The tiniest of tiny hamlets. No one in sight; but yes, a stout peasant woman, a huge basket on her head, is coming toward me. I stop her.

"Where is the church St. Genevieve?"

In voluble patois she directs me. I walk up the one long street, stone walls on each side hiding the houses. At the end, near an old fountain, I find the church I am seeking, and enter. An old woman who is telling her beads before an image of the Madonna, motions me to the door of the sacristy. I knock.

"Entrez," comes back. A tall form, a beaming face, a pleasant voice greet me. It is the Abbé Delaumosne.

"What can I do for you, my child?"

In a few words I state my errand. I wish to talk with him about Delsarte. He is greatly interested in the report I bring of the spread of Delsarte's teachings in America. He gives me the following resumé:

"François Delsarte was born Nov. 11, 1811, at Solesme, France. His father, a physician, died leaving his family poor. The young Delsarte was sent to Paris, in 1822, to study with a painter on china, but his tastes carried him into other channels. He became, in 1825, a pupil of the conservatory, a government institution for instruction in dramatic art, music, and the ballet. Here, for the want of proper guidance, he lost his voice. Finding himself thus incapacitated for the stage, he resigned that career for that of a teacher of singing and the dramatic art. Realizing that he had been shipwrecked for want of a compass and pilot, he determined to save others from his fate by seeking and formulating the laws of an art hitherto left to the caprice of mediocrity, or the inspiration of genius. After years of unremitting labor and study—study which took him by turns to hospitals, morgues, asylums, prisons, art galleries, etc., patiently unearthing the secrets and methods of past genius—study which kept him enchained by the hour watching the children at play in the great public gardens, weighing humanity everywhere and everyhow, he succeeded in discovering and formulating the laws of æsthetic science. Thanks to him, that science has now the same precision as that of mathematics. He died, without arranging his life-work for publication, July 20, 1871. Many are the names, famous in their different careers, that have owed much to his instruction—Rachel, Sontag, Pasca, Monsabre, etc."

We talked for some hours; then, late in the afternoon, I left, after promising a speedy return and renewal of our conversation.

This is an age of formulation. What Comte has done for exact science, Buckle and Mill for history, Spencer for culture, and Ruskin for painting, Delsarte has tried to do for action, for expression. It is as though the world, growing weary of productive activity, sought to pause and reärrange before plunging into further depths; to rescue from the void and formless mass of collected material a system whose symmetry and beauty should embody all that is worth saving; and, surely, an art like acting should have some higher standard than the empirical caprices of its exponents. "Trusting to the inspiration of the moment, is like trusting to a shipwreck for your first lesson in swimming."

In America, there is an opinion prevalent among actors, managers and the public at large to the effect that all work done on the stage should be the result of temperament rather than study; that if any study is given, it should be entirely personal, and should come from the actor's observation of his *own* emotions. More than this, they declare, is injurious, and will make one mechanical and elocutionary. They admit that, after one is fairly on the stage, a few things, such as standing, entrances and exits, points, taking the tone of one's interlocutor in a scene of excitement, etc., may be learned from old professionals. Now, I am not denying the great benefit to be derived from a careful study of one's own emotions; but how if one's personal experiences do not include the experience one is called upon to portray?

I was rehearsing "Phedre" one day to M. Regnier:—

"Recited with feeling," he criticised, "but you give me the love of a young girl, not that of a woman starving herself to death, and dying of remorse! Very well for Juliet, but it will not do for *Phedre*."

I had trusted to temperament and it had failed me.

Poets are born; but they have their laws of versification. Orators must study rhetoric; lawyers their codes; singers have a technique; musicians, harmony; painters, sculptors, architects,— all have some compass, some guide, which does not interfere with their natural aptitude, but only increases it. Things grow by what they feed on, and we save time by using the experiences of others.

A young painter shut himself in his studio, and laboriously worked out his own methods. One day he came forth jubilant, and imparted his discovery to Gerome.

"My dear boy," answered the master, "I could have showed you that in five minutes, and saved you two years of time!"

Delsarte has saved for the students of the dramatic profession many years of unnecessary labor; and to those who will faithfully and conscientiously follow his guidance, the result is certain, for he holds the lamp of truth.

Another great French master, Samson, has said:—
"*L'art c'est la naturel en doctrine érigé.*"

Many years ago an enthusiastic young man, finding himself in Paris in pursuit of art-studies, heard of the famous classes in pantomime of François Delsarte. He went, saw, and was conquered. He had found his master and the master his most ardent disciple—Steele Mackaye. The latter, like a John the Baptist, came back to America to prepare the New World for the coming of Delsarte. Talks, lectures, interviews in the daily papers on the grand new philosophy excited public attention, and prominent men united to bring Delsarte to this country. Visions of a conservatory, a theatre, and a reformed stage, which, like liberty, should enlighten the world, floated before the public gaze; and such people as William Stuart, of the old Winter Garden theatre, Alger, Monroe, thought the scheme practicable. But "man proposes and God disposes." The tocsin of battle was sounded, and France and Germany rushed into mortal combat. Delsarte could not leave his country, and before the angel of peace had descended on his troubled land, he had passed to the other world.

Decomposing Exercises.

LESSON I.

DECOMPOSING EXERCISES.

ÆSTHETIC TALK.

Dear pupil, will you accompany me, an invisible presence by my side, as we trace our way through a course of lessons? And if you practice faithfully, I can assure you that you will not regret the time and patience required in the study.

A lovely day in spring. You are before me. Listen to my words: The first great step in the study of this art is the attainment of perfect flexibility. This is acquired by diligent practice of the decomposing exercises, as witness:

I withdraw my will-power from fingers, then hand. Touch it. Do not shudder. Do you feel as if a dead thing had struck your living palm? Now I will show you the same phenomenon with forearm, entire arm, waist, spine, hips, knees, ankles, toes, jaw, eyelids. Now I fall. Give me your hand and help me to rise. I did not mean to startle you so. I have not even bruised myself. I simply withdrew my vital force into the reservoir at the base of the brain.

The first great thing to be acquired is flexibility of the joints. These exercises free the channels of expression, and the current of nervous force can thus rush through them as a stream of water rushes through a channel, unclogged by obstacles. We name these exercises *decomposing*. I wish you to buy a mirror large enough to reflect your entire figure, and faithfully to practice many hours a day if you wish rapid results.

Delsarte required of his pupils a great deal of hard work. You cannot in an instant prepare the human body for the translation, through that grand interpreter, art, of the best possibilities of the soul. There is too much imperfection in our nature.

The order of practice is as follows:

ÆSTHETIC GYMNASTICS.

1. Fingers;
2. Hand;
3. Forearm;
4. Entire arm;
5. Head;
6. Torso;
7. Foot;
8. Lower leg;
9. Entire leg;
10. Entire body;
11. Eyelids;
12. Lower jaw.

Exercise I.

Let fingers fall from knuckles as if dead; in that condition shake them. Vital force should stop at knuckles.

Exercise II.

Let hand fall from wrist as if dead; shake it in that condition forward and back, up and down, sideways, rotary shake.

DECOMPOSING EXERCISES. 13

Exercise III.

Drop forearm from elbow as if dead; shake it. Vital force arrested at elbow.

Exercise IV.

Raise arms above head, decompose them, *i. e.*, withdraw force. They will fall as dead weights. Arms still hanging decomposed from shoulders, agitate body with a rotary movement. The arms will swing as dead weights; now change and swing body forward and back; knee bends in this. The arms will describe a circle in their sockets; they must be decomposed.

Exercise V.

Drop head to one side decomposed; it will gradually describe a half-circle, moving from its own-weight as you have seen persons asleep nodding. Drop it back decomposed.

Exercise VI.

Drop torso sideways decomposed; commence with the head. The head will draw the shoulder; and, by degrees, with no conscious effort. the torso will fall. Do this first on one side, then on the other.

Exercise VII.

Lifting foot from the ground, agitate it as you do the hand. You better seat yourself for this exercise. Be sure the foot falls from the ankle decomposed.

Exercise VIII.

Decompose lower leg as forearm; agitate from knee.

Exercise IX.

(a.) Stand on footstool on one leg, then swing free leg by a motion of the entire body; free leg decomposed.

(b.) Lift leg from ground as a horse does in pawing, then drop it decomposed. You have discarded the footstool for the last exercise.

Exercise X.

Standing with your weight on back leg, bend that knee; also bend torso forward. The head should fall back. Withdraw the will from back leg; the body will drop to the ground.

Exercise XI.

Let lids fall as if going to sleep.

Exercise XII.

Let jaw fall so you feel its weight, *i.e.*, decomposed.

You must practice these exercises for me many hours a day; and, let me see—yes, come Thursday at two; you shall then teach me all this. I shall expect you to show me everything as if you know all and I nothing. Good morning.

Harmonic Poise of Bearing.

LESSON II.

HARMONIC POISE OF BEARING.

ÆSTHETIC TALK.

"*Art is at once the knowledge, the possession, and the free direction of the agents, by virtue of which are revealed the life, soul, and mind. It is the appropriation of the sign to the thing. It is the relation of the beauties scattered through nature to a superior type. It is not, therefore, the mere imitation of nature.*"

There, fellow-student, is not the above a succinct and beautiful definition of art, by the master Delsarte? I came across it the other day in Arnaud's book on Delsarte,* which, by the way, is very interesting. I advise you to read it; but beware of too much reading on the subject. You may then content yourself with the brain's knowledge; and what we are aiming for is unconscious cerebration, not conscious. The first is only acquired by a patient practice of the technique, as a singer studies her scales.

Remember, genius has been defined as "the power of taking great pains;" this, of course, united to a keen instinct. No study can take the place of natural intuition. Nature's voice must whisper to us our vocation, but study can prepare our instruments, perfect our tools. Cultivation can make the wild

---

* "Delsarte System of Oratory." By M. l'Abbé Delaumosne and Mme. Angelique Arnaud. $2. Edgar S. Werner, Publisher, 48 University Place, New York.

rose a Gloire de Dijon—a dream of beauty with its marvelous tinting and many petals delighting the eye, as its delicate perfume intoxicates the senses; but it cannot from a thistle make a rose. But, here, I am keeping you waiting; and you wish to commence your lesson.

ÆSTHETIC GYMNASTICS.

First take your weight on both feet, toes turned out, heels near together. A normal form will have the curves of a line of beauty, viz.: two convex curves separated and joined by a concave one. The head and leg form the convex curves, the torso forms the concave one, the head and the leg sympathizing.

Now, when by an act of will we change the weight so it no longer rests equally on both feet, we must always bear in mind the fact that the head sympathizes with the strong leg, that is, the head should incline to the side of the leg that bears the weight; while, as we observed above, the torso has an opposite curve from head and leg, and so should incline from the strong leg, thus always presenting nature's line of beauty.

Practice this now for me a few moments; I will call it off for you.

Attention!

Exercise I.

Stand firm on both legs.

Change weight, making right leg the strong one.

Incline head to right.

Incline torso to left.

You are now in a harmonic balance.

Incline torso to the right also and you become awkward; continue the inclination and you fall, thus proving the lack of equilibrium.

Oh, did you hurt yourself? Not much. That bruise will remind you to stand correctly; "it's an ill wind that blows no one good." Also let me warn you not to make the inclination of either head or torso too great; in other words, do not let them "flop;" a certain possession of the two in question is necessary for all dignity of attitude.

Attention!

Exercise II.

Stand firm, weight distributed equally on both legs.

Change weight, making left leg the strong one.

Incline head to the left, in accordance with the rule that the head must sympathize with the strong leg.

Incline torso to the right, in accordance with the rule that the torso should always be in opposition to the head and strong leg for perfect equilibrium.

Attention!

Exercise III.

Change slowly from left to right, keeping a perfect proportion of line during each second of the change.

Of course, the inclination of the head is more decided as is the torso when the weight is decidedly borne on one leg; it becomes less and less marked as you near the centre.

This opposition of the three parts of the body is one of the most beautiful things I know of. Hour after hour has flown by me unheeded as I examined one after another the exquisite forms of gods and heroes in the great museum of the Louvre; and no matter what the character the marble god portrayed, no matter what incident—battle or peace, pleasure or grief, anger or sorrow,—the god or hero showed his race by the divine lines of opposition. Those lines are ideal, and, of course, only in the ideal are they truth. They indicate a moral poise which *should* always be, but, alas! in our fallen human nature, is not always found. So some emotions, having in them no elements of the sublime, cannot be represented by the body in opposition.

Attention!

Exercise IV.

Stand with weight on both **legs.**

Advance one leg.

Carry the weight upon it. Advanced leg is now strong.

The head must incline forward in sympathy.

The torso must incline back.

This inclination of the torso hollows the back at the waist-line, and raises the chest. It is the attitude of the Apollo Belvedere.

HARMONIC POISE.

Incline torso forward in similar line to head and leg.

Ah! see, you throw out your hand for a support; left to yourself, you would totter and fall; so you see beauty is power.

Attention!

Exercise V.

Stand weight on both legs.

Place one leg behind you and carry the weight on to it.

Incline head back.

Incline torso forward.

Reverse that inclination of the torso and incline it in similar manner as the head, and the result will be as disastrous as in the former cases. I do not wish you to fall and hurt yourself; a slight tottering will prove the case as well as a tumble.

Attention!

Exercise VI.

From last attitude, viz., strong leg behind, sway gently forward until the weight is carried on to the forward leg.

Allow head and torso to sway gently in opposition as the centre of gravity changes.

The slowness with which the changes are made, taking care that the motion shall be continuous, is one of the principal things to observe after the inclinations of the head and torso are seen to be correct.

N. B.—The nervous control is of inestimable value; I advise a great deal of practice.

One has a sensation, in watching some one essaying the above, of being magnetized. The control of it enables the performer to show a most subtle attraction or repulsion, to change his weight from extreme front or back or side, to an opposite, without the observer seeing the change; he will only feel it, and it lends a magnetic charm to all change of bearing. Not that it should always be used—only in subtleties.

Attention!

Exercise VII.

Stand weight on both legs, feet together.

Sway gently forward until the weight is on the balls of the feet—the heels must not rise from the ground.

The head will incline slightly forward in sympathy with the forward weight. The torso will incline slightly back in opposition to the forward weight.

Attention!

Exercise VIII.

From above attitude sway gently back until weight is carried on to the heels—the toes must not rise from the ground.

The head will incline slightly back in sympathy with the back weight.

The torso will incline slightly forward in opposition to the back weight.

Continue it forward and back, forward and back, for some time.

Let me again enjoin on you to make the movement as slow as possible.

Ah! you feel mesmerized yourself, do you not? You take a long breath; it is a strange sensation. "There are more things in heaven and earth, Horatio, than are dreamed of in your philosophy."

Attention!

Exercise IX.

Stand weight on both feet, heels together, toes apart.

At waist-line rotate torso to the right, simultaneously rotating head to the left. Be careful that this rotation is made by the waist and not by the thighs.

Now reverse above, rotating torso to the left and head to the right.

I wish you to practice this for me until great flexibility has been secured at the waist. I cannot find words enough to express to you the great importance I lay upon this exercise. Almost all sinuousness depends on the easy control of the muscles at the waist. Without that control one may be gracious, but never graceful. All masters for the ballet insist on arduous work in this direction.

Delsarte writes: "*Dynamic wealth depends on the number of articulations brought into play;*" and also: "*When two parts follow the same direction, they cannot be simultaneous without an injury to the law of opposition;*" and the great articulation, so to speak, to learn to control is at the waist (though strictly it is not an articulation).

But you must be tired by this time; I have kept you standing a long time. You may now sit down and we will practice in a chair.

Attention!

Rotate waist and head as described above. Very well; you really are making remarkable progress. I wish all my pupils were as intelligent.

Attention!

Exercise X.

Seat yourself squarely.

Incline torso forward.

Incline head back. Make this movement a simultaneous one.

Now reverse above; *i. e.*, incline torso back as you incline head forward.

Practice this for me half a dozen times—one! two! three! four! five! six! There, there, you forget; your head is not moving in opposition. Yes, you are right now.

Attention!

Exercise XI.

Seat yourself as before.

Incline torso to the right; simultaneously incline head to the left.

Reverse this; *i. e.*, incline torso to the left as you incline head to the right.

Be careful in this last exercise that the torso is not forward or back. There, you see yours was bent back. We wish a direct side action.

Attention! Now we will make a combination:

Exercise XII.

Incline torso forward and to the right; simultaneously incline head back and to the left.

Reverse this; *i. e.*, incline torso forward and to the left; simultaneously incline head back and to the right.

I have already advised the use of a mirror, so I counsel you to give your reflection these lessons; and I beg of you to be strict with her or him.

Attention!

Exercise XIII.

Incline torso back and to the right; simultaneously incline head forward and to the left.

Reverse this; *i. e.*, incline torso back and to the left; simultaneously incline head forward and to the right.

Am I giving you too long a lesson? Remember, though, that you will have a whole month to perfect yourself in, and do not be impatient with me; we have nearly finished.

Attention!

Exercise XIV.

Combine the forward-side movement with a rotation of waist and head.

Very good.

Do the same with the back-side movement.

Perfect!

Attention!

Exercise XV.

Sway slowly, head and torso going in opposition, from extreme left to extreme right.

Reverse this; *i. e.*, sway slowly from extreme right to extreme left.

As I cautioned you when standing, make this movement as slow as you possibly can.

Attention!

Exercise XVI.

Sway gently from extreme back to extreme forward.

Take care—your head and torso are not moving in perfect opposition. That is better. You see the arc in which the head moves is a smaller one than that in which the torso moves. A perfect proportion, however, must be maintained.

Attention!

Exercise XVII.

Sway gently from back-left to forward-right, taking an oblique line. Oblique lines are always mystic.

Reverse this; *i. e.*, from forward-right sway slowly to back-left, still an oblique course.

In all of this never forget for one instant the simultaneous movement in opposition of the head and torso.

All the above is invaluable to the student who wishes a real harmonic poise of all the parts of the body.

ÆSTHETIC TALK—Continued.

Dear pupil, do you yet realize the meaning of the great word *study?* I hear reëchoing from the past,—
"You will arrive at no perfection in these and kindred exercises without spending many hours a day in arduous practice. There is no royal road. You should devote yourself heart and soul to this study. Shut the world away for a time; make no visits, receive no calls. A person who fritters away

her time in a thousand frivolous ways will accomplish nothing."

"An artist should be fit for the best society, and—keep out of it."—*Ruskin.*

All this was listened to with bated breath, and I *obeyed*. I was very young, and had great faith in my teacher; and faith is the corner-stone of the Temple of Art as well as of the Temple of God. I was unacquainted with the various discussions relative to the use and practicability of Delsarte's formulæ or his æsthetic gymnastics. I was like a child learning to spell, unconcerned as to the root of the words, as long as she went to the head of the class. The failure of many persons to physically demonstrate these theories comes, I have long fancied, from the lack of attention to the technique. They are fascinated by their analyzation; but when they try to put them into practice they find rebellious joints and stiffened muscles. Then they cry out: This is unnatural, studied; and so they return to their unconscious awkwardness. A little more practice and patience, and their acquired grace would have become unconscious.

I cannot be thankful enough that I was so constantly urged to practice, and was not allowed one advanced step until the preceding one was pronounced perfect; and if I stop and dwell on this here, dear invisible one, it is to call your attention to the great necessity for work; for there is but one step from the sublime to the ridiculous; and if, at the end of these lessons, you have not freed the channels for expression, you will simply be ridiculous, and will merit all the fun which is leveled at the mechanical mugging of so-called Delsarteans.

Work! work! work!

Basis of the System.

LESSON III.

PRINCIPLE OF TRINITY.

ÆSTHETIC TALK.

Good morning. Will you have a fan? It is much too warm for gymnastics. You shall show me your prowess later. For the present sit in this chair, by the open window. The air has been freshened by the shower. Look! A rainbow! It comes aptly to illustrate my talk.

Count the colors.

Red, orange, yellow, green, blue, indigo and violet —seven in all. Red, yellow and blue are the essential ones. The others are produced by overlapping.

Each primary color has its peculiar attribute distinct from the other two.

The red is the caloric, or heating principle.

The yellow is the luminous, or light-giving principle.

In the blue ray the power of actinism, or chemical action, is found.

The trinity of red, yellow and blue, when combined, constitute the unity of ordinary or white light. The three are one, the one is three.

Plants will blossom into a bright passion of life under the influence of the red and yellow rays. No fruit appears, however, without the added power of the blue ray. Life is unproductive until the three united in one bring all things to perfection.

Now, in that rainbow—ah! while we have been talking the "covenant of God" has faded away.

Come from the window, and look over my scrap-book with me.

"The number three was held sacred by the ancients, it being thought the most perfect of all numbers, as having regard to the beginning, middle and end."

The Druidical triad was infinite plentitude of life, infinite knowledge and infinite power—the three grand attributes of God.

God was first represented by the ancients under three principal forms, because goodness, wisdom and power are the three essential divine attributes; for instance: The Egyptians represented divine goodness by the god Osiris; the Greeks, by Jupiter; the Persians, by Oromazes. Divine wisdom was represented by the goddess Isis, in Egypt; by Pallas Athene, in Greece; and by Mythene, in Persia. The third principle was called by the Egyptians, Orus; by the Greeks, Apollo; and by the Persians, Mithas.

The oracle of Serapis said: "First God, then the Word and Spirit, all uniting in one whose power can never end."

While Pythagoras, the Samian philosopher, states that the symbol of all things or fulness is the monad, active principle, or father; the duad, passive principle, or mother; and the result or operation of both united.

The ancient trinities of the Hindoos, as well as those of the Egyptians, emblematized the male or paternal principle, the female or maternal principle, and the offspring. The same was done by early Chinese philosophy. The Chinese take the triangle to signify union, harmony,—the chief good of man, the heaven, the earth.

Numberless superstitions and confused notions

PRINCIPLE OF TRINITY.

were founded on the corruptions of this philosophy, as it became more debased and licentious.

In the philosophy of the ancient Egyptians, the first principle of the mind is said to be intellect; the second, will; and the third, which was the joint efflux of these, concord or harmony of action.

The Platonic hypothesis seems to be: Infinite goodness, infinite wisdom, and infinite active power, not as mere qualities or accidents, but as substantial things, all uniting to make up one divinity.

The above ideas agree with Swedenborg. He defines trinity as consisting of "love, wisdom and power. Love, being the origin and parent of all existence, is called Father; wisdom, which is the form of love, is named the Son, and the only begotten; while the divine power, consisting in the perfect union of love and wisdom, going forth in creative energy and life-imparting influence, is the Holy Spirit."

These are the sacred triune which form the fulness of the Godhead.

But you ask, "What has all this to do with dramatic expression or æsthetic gymnastics? I did not come here for a sermon."

Patience, you will soon see the connection. Every created thing is composed of two parts: a life-power or energy, and a form to show this power in effect. This demonstrates to us an important fact, namely, that there must be a union of two forms—one spiritual, the other material; the spiritual form being the life-power or energy, and the material form being the one which appears to the senses. The latter is the form by which life-power or energy is brought into action. Swedenborg writes:

"Three degrees: living endeavor, living power, and living motion. The endeavor in a man who is a living subject is his will united to his understanding; the living powers in him are what constitute the interior of his body, in all of which there are moving fibres variously interwoven; and living motion in him is action which is produced through those powers by the will united to the understanding. Powers have no potency but by action of the body."

Come to this long mirror with me. What do you see reflected?

Your own figure, yes; but do not yet turn away. Name for me the separate parts. Head, torso, legs and arms. Very well, but include legs and arms under one term,—limbs. Now, according to our philosophy, matter has no form of itself. It is being that forms the matter. That head, torso and limbs, which you have just named, are but the covering of a spiritual head, torso and limbs.

"It is sown a natural body; it is raised a spiritual body."

St. Paul says: "There is a natural body and there is a spiritual body." Notice: not an essence, but a formed body. Again, Swedenborg writes: "Man is a microcosm. His *esse* or soul corresponds to love; his *existere* is that which is called his body; it corresponds to wisdom; the proceeding from both is that which is called the sphere of his life— it is his power."

That interior head, torso and limbs are often very badly expressed by the outside covering, and cower abashed and ashamed at the representation given of them to the world.

To recapitulate the foregoing ideas:

All things exist from a first cause, deific essence. This essence is a trinity; an imperfect human correspondent and example being man, in whom the

Principle of Trinity. 35

trinity of faculties, will, understanding and memory, act together as one mind. The triune in deific essence is Love, Wisdom, Power.

Delsarte himself says:

"The principle of the system lies in the statement that there is in the world a universal formula which may be applied to all sciences, to all things possible.

"This formula is the trinity.

"What is requisite for the formation of a trinity?

"Three expressions are requisite, each presupposing and implying the other two. Each of the three terms must imply the other two. There must also be an absolute co-necessity between them. Thus, the three principles of our being, life, mind and soul, form a trinity.

"Why?

"Because life and mind are one and the same soul; soul and mind are one and the same life; life and soul are one and the same mind."

Delsarte employs the word *life* above as the equivalent of *sensation*, of physical manifestations.

Now, you may ask what has all this to do with dramatic expression; why go into the region of metaphysics?

Let me again recall to you,—

"Art is at once the knowledge, the possession,

and the free direction of the agents by virtue of which are revealed the life, soul and mind. It is the appropriation of the sign to the thing. It is the relation of the beauties scattered through nature to a superior type. It is not, therefore, a mere imitation of nature."

Now, man is the object of art. So you see we need a firm basis when we would have types—truth, —not a mere imitation of an often distorted nature.

In analyzing the organism, Delsarte stated that the inflection of the voice is the language of the sensitive nature, or physical life; gesture the language of emotion or soul; articulation the language of reason.

The first he named *vocal;* the second, *dynamic;* the third, *buccal*.

These languages correspond to the three states which art is to translate:

1. The sensitive state to the life;
2. The moral state to the soul;
3. The intellectual state to the mind.

"From the fusion of these three states in varying and incessant combination, and from the predominance of one of the primitive modalities, whether accidental or permanent, countless individualities are formed, each with its personal constitution, its shades of difference of education, habits, age, character, etc."

PRINCIPLE OF TRINITY. 37

I have quoted the above from Arnaud on Delsarte. However, do not be frightened at the vista opening before you. It is much simpler than you think. Again let me quote Arnaud:

"It is upon this mutual interpenetration of the various states in the triple unity, that the master founds the idea which dominates and pervades his whole system. * * * Three, the vital number, must, by its very essence and by inherent force, raise itself to its multiple nine. This is what the master calls the ninefold accord."

All motion is expansive which is objective, which has relation to the exterior world. So Delsarte has named motion from yourself as a centre, *excentric*.

Again we fold in, contract, concentrate our motion in subjective states of mind. So motion to a centre Delsarte has named *concentric*.

Motion between these two extremes, being well balanced, he has aptly termed *normal*.

In essence, reason is mental; will or love is moral or volitional; sensation or feeling is vital or physical; which three states of being are translated in the organism by the motions,—concentric for mental, normal for moral, excentric for vital.

Below is the chart of the ninefold accord. The late Prof. Monroe called it "the key of the universe."

He also called Delsarte "Swedenborg geometrized;" but we are wandering from our criterion.

"In appropriate language—wherein new words are not lacking for the new science—he takes apart each of the agents of the organism, enumerated above; he examines them in their details, and assigns them their part in the sensitive, moral, or intellectual transmission with which they are charged. Thus gesture—the interpreter of sentiment—is produced by means of the head, torso and limbs; and in the functions of the head are comprised the physiognomic movements, also classified and described, with their proper significance, such as anger, hate, contemplation, etc.,—and the same with the other agents. Each part observed gives rise to a special chart, where we see, for instance, what should be the position of the eye in exaltation, aversion, intense application of the mind, astonishment, etc. The same labor is given to the arms, the hands and the attitudes of the body, with the mark, borrowed from nature, of the slightest movement, partial or total, corresponding to the sensation, the sentiment, the thought that the artist wishes to express. I hope that these works may yet be recovered entire, for the master was lavish of them, and that they may be given to the public. Many of these papers were entrusted by the family to a former pupil of Delsarte, who took them to America."—*Arnaud on Delsarte.*

N. B.—**These charts are now presented to the public, complete, for the first time. The author has felt it almost in the light of a sacred duty to rescue the life-work of the great master Delsarte, from the threatening oblivion.**

CHART I.—CRITERION.

Essence. Mento-mental. Action. Concentro-concentric.	Essence. Moro-mental. Action. Normo-concentric.	Essence. Vito-mental. Action. Excentro-concentric.
Essence. Mento-moral. Action. Concentro-normal.	Essence. Moro-moral. Action. Normo-normal.	Essence. Vito-moral. Action. Excentro-normal.
Essence. Mento-vital. Action. Concentro-excentric.	Essence. Moro-vital. Action. Normo-excentric.	Essence. Vito-vital. Action. Excentro-excentric.

A good shorthand of these terms is made by the use of the grave accent (\ ), such as is employed over French vowels, for the name concentric; an acute accent (/) for the name excentric; a dash (—) for the name normal. For the ninefold accord combine.

On the seashore, the other day, I saw some darkies running a bag-race. A sack is tied about the neck, confining the body. In this guise each unfortunate racer struggles to run. It reminded me of man: his spirit is imprisoned, incarnated. We chain it stronger by an education, teaching that all expression is vulgar.

The caste of " Vere de Vere " must be impassive. Æsthetic gymnastics aim to break that chain—no more. They will not dower you with soul. That is God-given. And here, dear pupil, a hint. Cultivate your mind and heart. For the expression of noble emotions, one must feel noble emotions. You can never show truly more than you are capable of experiencing. Imitation will carry you but a short way. Personification contains the Promethean spark.

In the museum of the Louvre is seen the original Venus of Milo. Other art-galleries must content themselves with a copy. The beautiful marble woman, an inner spirit, is clothed in plaster. Her lovely head, torso and limbs shape it to a semblance of herself. The inner Venus, like the spiritual body, is the form, as the idea of the sculptor was first the form of the marble goddess.

Take pencil and paper, and write what I dictate.

Principle of Trinity.

The human body has three grand divisions:
1. Head = mental or intellectual;
2. Torso = moral or volitional;
3. Limbs = vital or physical.

Each division subdivides into parts. The zones are significant points of arrival or departure for the gesture.

The head has three active and three passive zones. The active zones are:
1. Frontal = mental;
2. Buccal = moral or volitional;
3. Genal = vital.

The passive zones are:
1. Temporal = mental;
2. Parietal = moral or volitional;
3. Occipital = vital.

The torso contains three zones:
1. Thoracic = mental;
2. Epigastric = moral or volitional.
3. Abdominal = vital.

The arm has three sections:
1. Hand = mental;
2. Forearm = moral or volitional;
3. Upper arm = vital.

The leg has three sections:
1. Foot = mental;

2. Lower leg = moral or volitional;

3. Upper leg or thigh = vital.

The articular centres of the arm are three:

1. The shoulder = a thermometer of passion (the word passion here signifies impulse, excitement, vehemence);

2. The elbow = a thermometer of the affections and self-will;

3. The wrist = a thermometer of vital energy.

Have you finished copying? You do not understand it thoroughly? Well, we will see if a little talk and some few examples will elucidate matters.

No, don't fold away your paper. Look over it again. What did you first write?

1. "Head = mental or intellectual." Surely that explains itself. The common phrase of "he has no head," reminds us that head corresponds to mind.

2. "Torso = moral or volitional." Volitional signifies pertaining to the will, the desires, the love of the being. The torso contains the two great motive organs of the body—the heart and lungs.

3. "Limbs = vital or physical." Powerful action, progression, deeds,—all depend on the limbs. How familiar the expression, "He stretched forth his arm," or, "The protecting arm of his country," to signify power.

Now we come to the zones.

PRINCIPLE OF TRINITY. 43

The head, which, as a division, is mental, contains, however, in that mental three active and three passive zones, modifying the division:

1. "Frontal = mental." If I had a black-board here I would draw a head for you. Lacking it, we must imagine one. The frontal zone includes the forehead and eyes. "The mental eye;" "a clear-sighted man"—one whose understanding is clear; we "look" into a subject; we "see" a reason; we refer to various degrees of illumination, of blindness, darkness and brilliancy in reference to the intellect, —all of which illustrates the frontal zone as purely mental.

2. "Buccal = moral or volitional." Buccal means pertaining to the cheek. This zone includes the cheek and nose. "A keen-scented man" refers to one whose perceptions are keen. The nose reveals the will or desire. The noses of different nations reveal the leading desire of that nation, viz.: The Roman nose, conquest, cruelty; the Greek nose, ethics, beauty; the Turk's nose, sensuality, etc.

3. "Genal = vital." Genal comes from an old French word, meaning pertaining to the mouth or chin. The mouth is contained in this zone. Now, a mouth-zone represents touch, taste and sound. All three are vital.

The above-named zones are capable of many more subdivisions.

The base of the brain is vital. Reference is often made to a man's thick neck, when we call attention to an overpreponderance of the physical. The middle of the head, when high, indicates reverence. It is the moral zone. The front brain is mental.

There is a certain amount of truth in physiognomy and phrenology; and the student of expression will find an added interest in life by scrutinizing the faces and heads of chance acquaintances. Many a moment has passed unheeded as, seated in the cars settled for a long ride, I have amused myself in constructing character and life from stories told by the faces opposite.

Look again on your paper.

"The torso contains three zones.

1. "Thoracic = mental." The lungs are more in that region than in the lower zone. Lungs are mental. Their action we name inspiration, aspiration, expiration, etc. We also say the same of the mind. They purify the blood, as truth does the will or love.

2. "Epigastric = moral or volitional," pertaining to the love of the being. This zone contains the heart, an organ always used in metaphor as expressive of love. The feelings largely affect the action of this organ. It beats quicker in excitement, slower

in fear or horror. Our entire being is affected by a change in its normal action. It feeds with its life-giving fluid all our body, as love feeds, governs and directs our being. The moral zone is the affectional zone. Gestures directed from that section, as a point of departure, express love as the side of the being preponderating in expression.

3. " Abdominal = vital." This zone, as a point of arrival or departure for the gesture, is called vital, as representing the more material, physical instincts. Gestures proceeding from this section are vulgar or sensual.

You are not forgetting, I hope, that, as a division, the torso is moral or volitional, representative of the desire of the being. Never lose sight of the grand division. It exerts a modifying influence on the subdivision.

Three sections in the arm. Read them from your paper:

1. " Hand = mental." The hand emphasizes the expression of the eyes. The eyes are mental. The hand is mental in the grand vital division of the arm. The eye looks toward an object, the hand points. We talk with the hand to the deaf and dumb. We write with the hand; we draw, play, work with the

hand. Need more be adduced to show it the agent of the brain?

2. "Forearm = moral or volitional." Samson, the great French actor and teacher, writes: "The elbow is the soul of the arm." It is the articulation connecting the upper arm vital, with the forearm moral.

3. "Upper arm = vital." Vital force flows first from the brain into that section. "Strike out from the shoulder," is a familiar phrase. There can be no force in the arm if the muscles of that portion are undeveloped.

Read the next.

1. "Foot = mental." Have you never observed a person in thought tapping his foot on the floor? The foot makes gestures as the hand does. It advances, retreats, stamps and—kicks!

2. "Lower leg = moral or volitional." We kneel in the expression of reverence, love, obedience, etc., whenever we would express a subordination of our will to that of others. This brings the moral section of the leg into prominence.

3. "Upper leg or thigh = vital." Like the upper arm, the vital impelling force flows first into this part. No powerful action of the legs is possible without muscle being developed there. *The first*

impulse of the leg in walking should be felt in the thigh.

Will you read me the next?

"The articular centres of the arm are three."

1. "The shoulder = a thermometer of passion—"

Please hand me that book. Take your pencil and copy these extracts from Delsarte's notes:

"I reproduced the movements of the head, but they were awkward and lifeless. What was the cause? As I uttered the preceding words, I noticed that under the sway of the grief which dictated them, my shoulders were strangely lifted up; and, as then I found myself in the attitude which I had previously tried to render natural, the unexpected movement of my shoulders had suddenly impressed it with an expression of justice and truth. Thus I gained possession of an æsthetic fact of the first rank.

"The shoulder intervenes in all forms of emotion. What, then, shall I call it? What name shall we give to its dominant rôle—'thermometer,' I cried; there is an excellent word! The shoulder is, in fact, precisely the thermometer of passion as well as of sensibility; it is the measure of their vehemence; it determines their degree of heat and intensity. However, it does not specify their nature. The thermometer marks the degrees of heat and cold without specifying the nature of the weather.

"The shoulder, in rising, is not called upon to teach us whether the source of the heat or violence which mark it arises from love or hate. It belongs to the face to show that. Now, the shoulder is limited; first, that the emotion expressed by the face is or is not true; then in marking with mathematical rigor the degree of intensity to which that emotion rises. The shoulder, in every man who is moved or actuated, rises sensibly, his will playing no part in the ascension. The shoulder is, therefore, a thermometer of sensibility."

Delsarte goes on to state that people of the higher classes have a gamut of expression subtler than those of the lower; still, in a degree, the shoulder rises even with them when they are under the influence of real emotion. With them it is the law of infinitesimal quantities. There must be a difference between "the swift and flexible movements of an elegant organism and those evolutions clumsily executed by the torpid limbs hardened by constant labor."

I have let Delsarte himself explain his reason for calling the shoulder a thermometer of sensibility.

2. "The elbow = a thermometer of the affections

and self-will." I quoted Samson above: "The elbow is the soul of the arm." In its movement toward an object, if the forearm and hand continue the direction, the action expresses affection to the object. If the hand is brought back, for instance, akimbo, it is self-assertive affection for yourself. It is thus a thermometer of the affections.

3. "The wrist = a thermometer of vital energy." The arm, as a whole, is a vital division. The vital energy is concentrated or exploded from the wrist.

The hip, knee and ankle do not need dwelling on. The hip thrown out, indicates vulgarity, sensualism; the knee, assertion; the ankle concentrates vital energy as the wrist does.

To impress the foregoing zones well on your mind, practice the following. I will call off:—

ÆSTHETIC GYMNASTICS.

Exercise I.

Place your hand on your forehead, the mental zone, and say:
"There's a fearful thought!"

Exercise II.

Take your hand away from your forehead, using that zone as a point of departure for the gesture, and say:
"I will not entertain so bad a thought!"

Exercise III.

Place your hand on your cheek, the moral or affectional zone, and repeat:

"Oh, Romeo, Romeo, wherefore art thou Romeo!"

You remember Romeo says: "See, how she leans her hand upon her cheek."

Exercise IV.

Take your hand away from the cheek with a little gesture of negation, and repeat:

"Deny thy father!"

Exercise V.

Place your chin in the palm of your hand and say:

"I shall forget to have thee still stand there, remembering how I love thy company!"

Exercise VI.

With the tips of the fingers throw a kiss taken from the mouth:

"A thousand times good night!"

In the head, whatever may be the distinctive zone, it is mentalized.

Exercise VII.

Place your hand on the brain, near the forehead, and repeat:

"Well, Juliet, I will lie with thee to-night. Let's see for means!"

Exercise VIII.

Carry the hand from that zone, and repeat:
"I do remember an apothecary!"

Exercise IX.

Place your hand on the top of your head, on the bump of reverence, as phrenologists would say, and repeat:
"It is even so!"

Exercise X.

Carry the hand from that zone, and repeat:
"Then I defy you, stars!"

Exercise XI.

Place your hand at the back of the brain, the vital zone, and repeat:
"'Tis torture and not mercy. Heaven is here where Juliet lives."

Exercise XII.

Place your hands on the chest, the mental zone, in the affectional division, the seat of honor, and repeat:
"To live an unstained wife to my sweet love."

Exercise XIII.

Carry the hands out from chest and repeat:
"Shall I speak ill of him that is my husband?"

Exercise XIV.

Place your hand on your heart, the moral or affectional zone, and repeat:
"Or this true heart with treacherous revolt turn to another."

Exercise XV.

Carry the hands from heart and repeat:
"Take all myself."

Exercise XVI.

Place your hand on your abdomen, the vital zone, and repeat:
"My poverty, not my will, consents."

His poverty is starvation, a vital physical feeling; so, in taking the money Romeo offered, his hand departs from that vital zone.

Exercise XVII.

Carry the hand from the abdomen. The apothecary does so to receive the gold. Gestures of affection, departing from that zone, are sensual. One slaps the thigh as a vulgar expression of vital satisfaction; kneels in reverence or love; stamps the foot in mental excitement.

(*a.*) Repeat as you slap the thigh:
"Gregory, on my word, we'll not carry coals."

(*b.*) Repeat as you kneel:
"O, speak again, bright angel!"

(c.) Repeat as you stamp the foot:
   "Wilt thou provoke me! Then have at the boy."

Now, I think, dear pupil, you have quite a budget to study for me during the next month. Of course, it will need patience and perseverance on your part. It is very difficult, almost impossible, to do without the aid of a living teacher. Greater industry will be needed on your side. Good-bye, we shall meet again when the leaves are red and gold, in the beautiful month of October.

Vital Division.

LESSON IV.

THE LEGS.

ÆSTHETIC TALK

Good day. Will you have this bunch of goldenrod? Let me fasten it in your dress, an autumn greeting. I have come from a walk through the fields, and purple aster, and red sumach, and goldenrod look up to the grey-tinted sky. Have you made as much progress in your work as nature has in hers? Think of it! When first we met in June, the meadows were one white plain of daisies, earth's stars; now they seem to have drawn the glowing sunset tints into their fecund bosom, and sent them, quivering with life, upward into passionate blossoming.

What shall we study to-day? Draw your chair to the table; there you will find pen and paper. Copy as I dictate from our master Delsarte:

"Æsthetics is the science of the sensitive and passional manifestations which are the object of art, and whose psychic form it constitutes.

"Semeiotics is the science of the organic signs by which æsthetics must study inherent fitness.

"The object of art, therefore, is to reproduce, by the action of a superior principle (ontology), the organic signs explained by semeiotics, and whose inherent fitness is estimated by æsthetics.

"If semeiotics does not tell us the passion which the sign reveals, how can æsthetics indicate to us the sign which it should apply to the passion that it studies? In a word, how shall the artist translate the passion which he is called upon to express?

"Æsthetics determines the inherent forms of sentiment in view of the effects whose truth of relation it estimates.

"Semeiotics studies organic forms, in view of the sentiment which produces them.

"To sum up:

"1. If, from a certain organic form, I infer a certain sentiment, that is *Semeiotics*.

"2. If, from a certain sentiment, I deduce a certain organic form, that is *Æsthetics*.

"3. If, after studying the arrangement of an organic form whose inherent fitness I am supposed to know, I take possession of that arrangement under the title of methods, invariably to reproduce that form by substituting my individual will for its inherent cause, that is *Art*.

"4. If I determine the initial phenomena under the impulsion of which the inherent powers act upon the organism, that is *Ontology*.

"5. If I tell how that organism behaves under the inherent action, that is *Physiology*.

THE LEGS. 59

"6. If I examine, one by one, the agents of that organism, it is *Anatomy*." *

Let us consider the third paragraph.

"The object of art, therefore, is to reproduce, by the action of a superior principle (ontology), the organic signs explained by semeiotics, and whose inherent fitness is estimated by æsthetics."

Look with me at this aster. Do you realize that the purple star is as much the result of its "superior principle" as you or I am of ours?

The spirit in a plant is its power of gathering from the earth and the air dead matter, and shaping it to its chosen form. The flower is the sign, the end, the creature, that the spirit makes.

You see, then, dear pupil, two things to observe: One the life-power and energy; the other, the form proceeding therefrom, and most perfectly adapted to bring them into outward manifestation.

What we produce is merely the form of what exists in our minds. Every stroke of the artist's brush is made within ere it glows on the canvas. In the actor, every accent, every inflection, every gesture, is but the outer reverberation of the still small voice within.

---

* Arnaud on Delsarte.

The idea, as separate from the object, exists prior to the object itself; and the outward work is but the material form, the effect of the spiritual idea or spiritual form.

> "The certain and practical sense of this word 'spirit.' The sense in which you all know that its reality exists as the power which shaped you into shape, and by which you love and hate when you have received that shape. You need not fear, on the one hand, that either the sculpturing or the loving power can ever be beaten down by the philosophers into a metal, or evolved by them into a gas; but, on the other hand, take care that you yourselves, in trying to elevate your conception of it, do not lose its truth in a dream or even in a word. The 'spirit of man' truly means his passion and virtue, and is stately according to the height of his conception, and stable according to the measure of his endurance."—*Ruskin*.

Delsarte says:

"*External gesture, being only the reverberation of interior gesture, which gives it birth and rules it, should be its inferior in development.*"

He adds:

"*A voice, however powerful it may be, should be inferior to the power which animates it.*"

After reflecting seriously on the foregoing, how can one call the system of Delsarte mechanical? Do we consider the blossoming into beauty of a rose mechanical because we soften and sod the hard soil through which it must force itself into being? We make the ground flexible for the tender rootlets, as we aim to make the clay of which we are made plastic to the inner emotion, revelatory of the soul. The music of the spheres might be echoing in the brain of some inspired master; but without an instrument how could he convey its wondrous vibrations to his fellow-souls?

Ontology deals with the inner impelling power, the individual will. Suppose I say in metaphor, "The Greeks achieved marvelous deeds, nurturing the gifts of the intellect like faithful gardeners, and making them bring forth marvelous fruit!"

Æsthetics would determine the fitness of the simile, semeiotics would determine the sign.

The science of semeiotics is the science of signs, of correspondences. Correspondence is derived from three Latin words, *cor-re-spondeo*, and it means literally *to answer again from the heart*. We use the word in common speech to show that written communication has passed between two people. It is only complete when the one written to has replied, has spoken to the other again *from the heart*. I am thus particular because a great deal is learned by a strict attention to the derivation of words.*

The material form should correspond to the inner form, should answer "thought to thought, heart to heart." "Correspondence is no arbitrary relationship like metaphor or figure, but one founded alike on the inward and outward nature of the things by which we are surrounded."

---

* "*Correspondence*, compounded of two Latin words *con*, with and *respondere*, to answer. Some have thought that correspondence might be more properly derived from *cor*, the heart, and *respondens*, answering; but as the signification is the same either way it is of little consequence."—*Science of Correspondences:* REV. EDWARD MADELEY.

I see an outward manifestation, viz., a child laughs. I infer that the child is pleased; it cries, I know it is displeased. Remember,—

"If, from a certain organic form, I infer a certain sentiment, that is semeiotics." An example of which is the foregoing.

"If, from a certain sentiment, I deduce a certain organic form, that is æsthetics."

An artist wishes to model Coriolanus exiled from Rome by the people for whom he had risked his life and shed his blood. Æsthetics would select the bearing, attitude, and expression. The marble must reveal the passion surging in the breast of the outraged hero.

Do you not now see at a glance the importance to the aspirant for dramatic laurels of a knowledge of semeiotics and æsthetics? The two, combined with individual will, make art.

I have dwelt at some length on the inherent principle, as I wished you never to lose sight of the fact that

"The spirit quickens, the letter kills."

In a science monthly of last year, I read an interesting account of the hypnotic experiments made by French doctors. A gendarme, on guard in front of the Louvre, was selected (on account of his phlegm) for the experiment. Thrown into a mesmeric sleep by means of a few passes, an artist,

THE LEGS. 63

summoned from a neighboring studio, posed him as a model of fear. The unconscious soldier obeyed the artist's hand. But now comes the strangest fact. He *felt* the emotion, and described himself as experiencing the throes of terror.

This seems to bear out an idea to be inculcated in these lessons, viz.: A perfect reproduction of the outer manifestation of some passion, the giving of the outer sign, will cause a reflex feeling within.

This is delicate ground, and will make some of you cry, "Mechanical." I feel like replying with Aunt Betsy Trotwood, "Donkeys, Janet, donkeys!" Think seriously a moment. Certain attitudes, by extending or contracting the muscles, by compelling the breath to come and go more rapidly, by increasing the heart-beats, cause physical interior sensations which are the correspondences of emotion. The emotion is then slightly felt, but you must bear in mind that the sign is first formed within; so, after all, the exterior expression does not come first. In the mesmerized subject, the idea was in the artist's mind. I am treading on egg-shells here, I am conscious.

The artistic idea within must form the outward expression, but that idea seems in genius to be unconscious; you cannot mentally plan it at the moment of its execution. Regnier said to me, in speaking of Delsarte: "If you have to seek in the head what ought to be in the heart, you are not an artist." That is true in itself, but not true of Delsarte. The latter may be mystical, he is certainly not mechanical. I think we shall find the solution in this:

All our study, all our observations, all our experiences, all our life, is mixed in the mystic alembic, which, for want of a clearer name, I will call our *interior memory*,—that unconscious storehouse where inherited tendencies, traits, and aptitudes are also found. At the call of art this memory awakes from its lethargy, and, without your having to again feel the emotion, forms the expression, which expression affects you in a reflex wave.

St. Augustine says: "Give me a lover and he will understand." And I say: "Give me a student with *feu sacre*, and he will understand."

How I have wandered! But, although these paths lead from the main road, they must be traversed by art's pilgrim, if he would know all the truth.

But to return. Semeiotics is thus the science of signs, and so the science of the form of gesture.

There are three types to be considered in man:
1. Constitutional;
2. Passional;
3. Habitual.

The constitutional type is that which is congenital.

The passional type is that produced under the sway of emotion.

The habitual type is one not inborn, but created by habit, which acts as a second nature, refashioning the material being.

Passional types explain habitual types, and habitual types explain congenital types.

Thus we obtain a complete analysis of man.

There are three forms of expression for gesture:
1. The habitual bearing of the agent of expression;
2. The emotional attitudes of the agent;
3. The passing inflections of the agent.

The bearing is the most permanent.

The attitudes are less so.

The inflections are passing.

Have you not observed how a man's habits will color his every action? This is such a well-recognized fact that we often hear. "He tried to pass for a gentleman, but his bearing betrayed him;" or, *vice versa*, "He disguised himself as a workingman and went among the people, but his habit of command betrayed him."

Continued indulgence in any one form of feeling will make that feeling the predominant trait. So beware, young sculptors, each day you are perhaps carving for — eternity.

Take your pencil again, and draw a chart containing nine squares similar to the one in our second lesson. Leave room in each square for writing the signification of the attitudes of the legs. Now lay your chart aside while you again listen.

The legs and arms form the vital division of the body, representing, as they do, the power of action.

Strong leg signifies that the weight of the body is borne on that leg.

Free leg signifies that the leg is free from weight.

Ex. is an abbreviation of *excentric*, *con.* for *concentric*, *nor.* for *normal*.

ÆSTHETIC GYMNASTICS.

Will you stand? I will call off the attitudes of the legs.

Attention!

Exercise I.—Action nor.-nor.

Both legs strong and wide apart; standing in the breadths, knees straight.

Signification: Vital repose, vulgarity, intoxication, fatigue. You see, one must always observe two things: An attitude may be a sign of a physical condition, or of a sentiment. The foregoing attitude indicates either a condition or a sentiment: A condition of fatigue, vertigo, or intoxication; or a sentiment of familiarity or vulgar boorishness.

THE LEGS. 67

A gentleman, in the privacy of his own household, might permit himself to stand, his hands under his coat-tails, his back to the fire in the nor.-nor. attitude. He would be a vulgar boor if he assumed the same position in society.
Attention!

Exercise II.—Action con.-nor.

Standing in the breadths; both legs are strong and together; knees straight, that is unbent; heels together; toes turned out.

N. B.—In all of these attitudes the toes should turn out.

This attitude signifies a condition of feebleness, or a sentiment of respect It is the one a child assumes, a valet, a soldier.

Gentlemen, in a formal introduction to ladies, or to those superior to themselves in station, take this position. It is taught to small cavaliers in dancing-school, when, with bent head and proffered arm, they beg their little sweethearts to tread a measure.

The young should always assume it before the old. It is the position of the inferior before the superior.
Attention!

Exercise III.—Action ex.-nor.

Standing in the lengths; both legs are strong and apart, one directly in front of the other; the knees are straight.

Do you observe that in all the normal attitudes of the legs, the weight is born equally on both ?

The condition signified is indecision, while the sentiment is deliberation. It is an action half-way between advance and retreat. A slight forward impetus would decide for advance, a slight backward movement would declare for retreat. A change of weight, however, would be necessary to indicate these two opposites. This attitude is agnostic,—it decides for nothing, but hesitates and cries, "Who knows?"

Attention!

Exercise IV.—*Action nor.-con.*

Standing in the lengths; the back leg is strong; the knee of that leg is straight; the forward leg is free, while its knee is bent, thus bringing the foot in front near to the foot behind.

N. B.—You will observe that in all three of the concentric attitudes, the weight is borne on the back leg. It is the final term which names the genus of the attitude. The first term serves as an attribute making a species in the genus.

The foregoing attitude signifies calm strength, reserved force, reflection, controlled emotions. It is an attitude which shows the mind as ruler, the attitude of the thinker, the scholar, the gentleman. It indicates concentration.

Attention!

Exercise V.—*Action con.-con.*

Standing in the lengths; the strong leg is back, its knee bent; the free leg is in front, the knee straight.

The condition shown is prostration; the sentiment, despondent passion.

Attention!

Exercise VI.—Action ex.-con.

Standing in the lengths; the strong leg is back, its knee straight; the free leg in front, the knee also straight.

The condition such a position represents is antagonistic; the sentiment, defiance, irritation, splenetic emotion.

It also indicates self-assertion with an added element of defiance.

Many men erroneously consider this position a manly one to assume. Remember, these attitudes are types. They can run into each other, mix, overlap, as colors in the rainbow. An attitude midway between the nor.-con. and the ex.-con. is very common. The mixed attitude, then, partakes of the meaning of the two from which it is composed.

Attention!

Exercise VII.—Action nor.-ex.

Standing in the lengths; strong leg is in front. Stand so firmly on the forward leg that the other is unnecessary for support; the knee is straight; free leg is behind, the knee bent; the ball of the foot rests on the ground; the heel should be raised.

This attitude signifies a condition of vigor, animation, intention, or attention. It represents sentiments of an ardent or passional tendency.

There is no introspection in this attitude, it is essentially excentric.

Attention!

Exercise VIII.—*Action con.-ex.*

Standing in the breadths; the free leg is slightly in the rear of the strong leg; the knee of the strong leg is straight; the free knee is bent; the toe of the free leg is on a line with the instep-arch of the strong leg; the foot of the free leg is very much turned out; the heel of the free leg is raised a little from the ground, while the ball rests on the ground.

The attitude should be unconstrained. It represents a suspensive condition, neutral, transitive, or colorless sentiments. It should be assumed when changing the direction of the lateral walk on the stage.

Attention!

Exercise IX.—*Action ex.-ex.*

Standing in the lengths; both legs should be wide apart; strong leg in front, the knee bent; free leg behind, the knee straight; the heel of the foot is raised, the ball resting on the ground.

This signifies a condition of great excitement or exaltation, sentiments of an explosive nature.

You have done very well. Practice these attitudes before a mirror, strictly observing a harmonic bearing in each of them.

Keep in mind your previous lesson on that subject, viz.: The head must sympathize with the strong leg, must incline to the side of the strong leg, while the torso inclines in the opposite direction, thus always preserving equilibrium and the line of beauty.

.ESTHETIC TALK.—Continued.

Again I will unearth some of my treasures for you. Look over my shoulder at this collection of photographed statues. We will select one for each of the foregoing attitudes.

See, here is a faun holding a huge bunch of grapes, high over head. With upturned face he is dropping them one by one into his laughing mouth. One seems to share the grapes, so contagious is his enjoyment. Be quick, be quick, my faun. Do I not hear the songs of the wine god and his bacchantes? Soon you must join their revelry. Still he stands in marble silence. Can you tell me in what attitude? Yes, correct, in the nor.-nor.. that of vital repose.

What have you found? Ah, Hebe, the bewitching little waitress on Olympus. She stands, with both lovely arms upraised. Her two dear little feet nestle close together. It is our second attitude.

Here in this frieze of the Parthenon we find our third example. That beautiful youth in the procession turns and stops for one short instant. About what does he hesitate? His lips are dumb — we shall never know.

Pallas Athene, haughty child of Zeus, reflection,

control, reserve power is conveyed by your bearing. You do not need Medusa of the snaky locks on your helmet to chill our blood. It freezes at your look. We enter your temple to worship, and Cupid and Bacchus are left outside, twining their garlands of roses and grapes.

Ariadne, do not despair. The same wind that is filling the sails of Theseus, and wafting his argosy from you, brings to your ear the chant of merry bacchantes. A hero has deserted, but a god comes to console. So courage. She still is despairing; the pictured stone changes not. She teaches us the fifth attitude.

Ah! Demosthenes, my noble friend, well met; but why this defiant position? Why this self-assertion? You have been petrified in the midst of an oration and are there to illustrate our sixth attitude.

"The horn of the hunter is heard on the hill." Diana! Diana of the Louvre! quick, select your arrow, shoot your bow. My heart beats quicker, my blood bounds at the sight of your vital presence. I would be one of your nymphs, Diana! Diana!

Sweet Modesty. Chastely your robes fold around you; you stand in a neutral attitude. What shall I judge from that?

Ah! Fighting gladiator! you indicate to me explosion, with your excited air and forward-bent knee. I am told that you are striving to seize the bridle of rearing horses with that outstretched arm, and you are running, not fighting. You have been much maligned.

What is it, child? You would look at the others? Seek some gallery where you will find casts of the antique, and spend a profitable hour in discovering the attitude in which each statue stands. Then go home and essay them before the glass.

CHART II.—

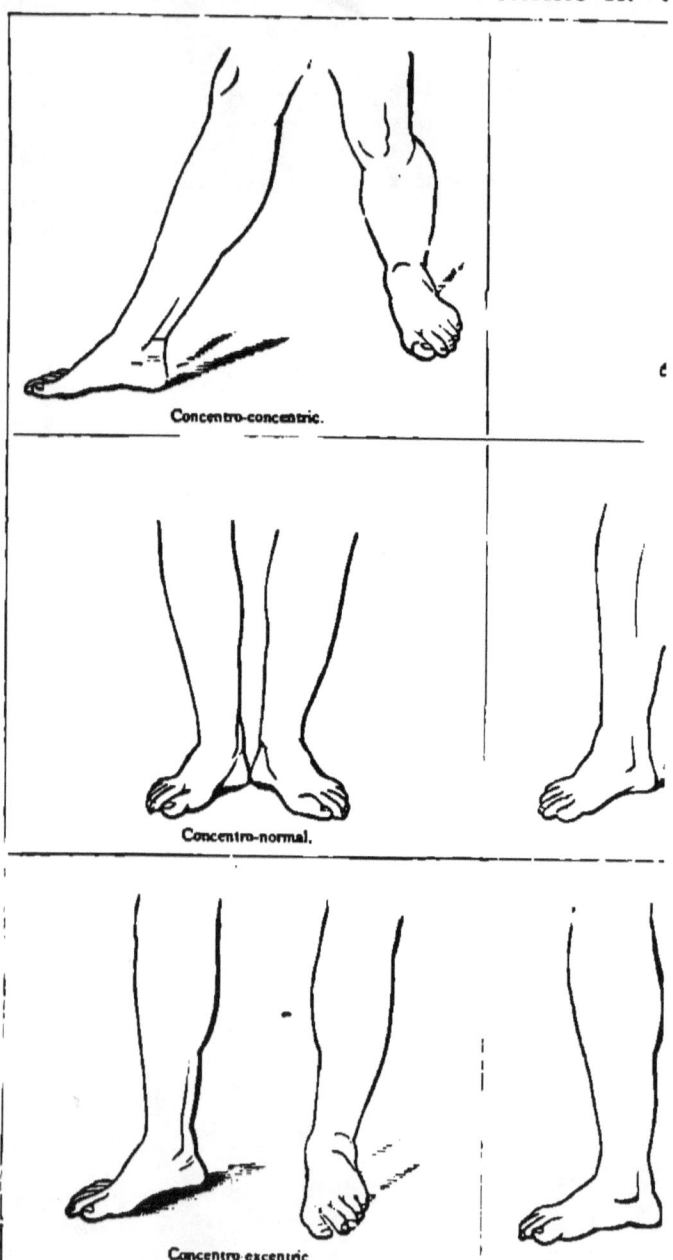

OF THE LEGS.

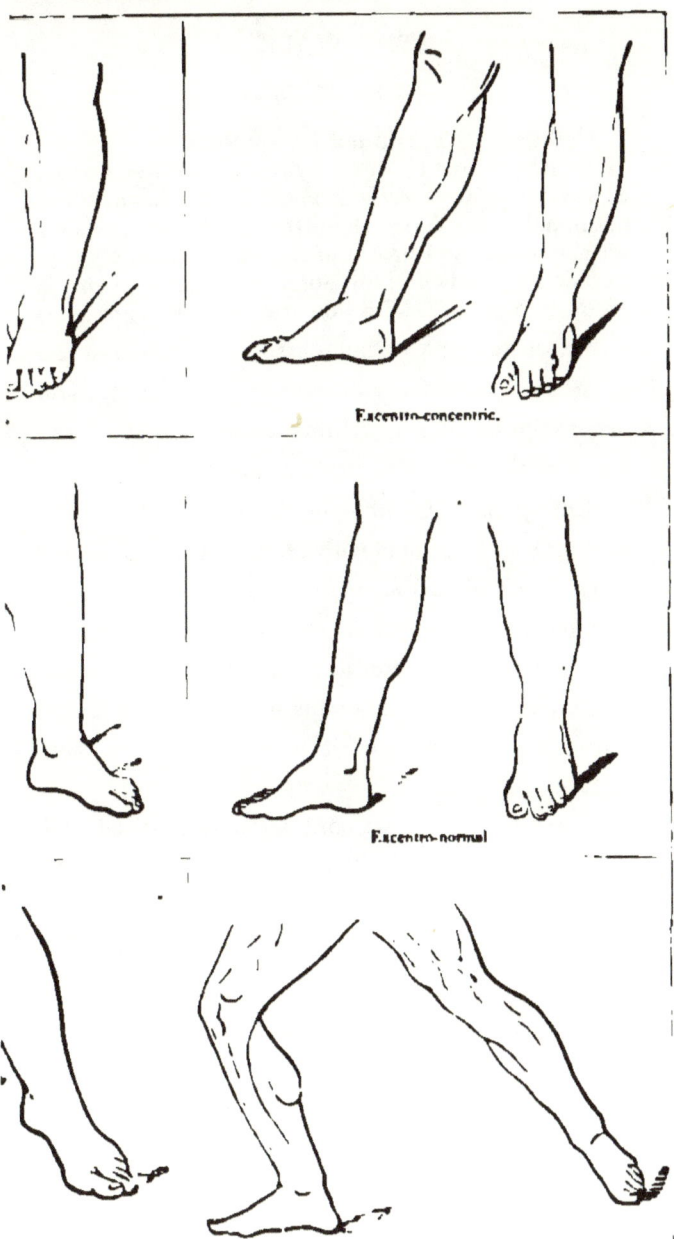

Excentro-concentric.

Excentro-normal.

Excentro-excentric.

LESSON V.

THE WALK.

ÆSTHETIC TALK.

Well met. Nay, do not lay off your hat; we will go to school in the woods, *faire l'école buissiniere*, as they say in *la belle* France. How keen is the autumnal air! A few hundred yards before us we see the scarlet and brown of the trees in hectic glory, frescoed against the blue dome of the sky. This is Madison Square. Will you rest on this bench?

We are out for a walking-lesson. For the last few moments I have been observing you intently, you unconscious. Are you brave enough to stand the fire of criticism? Your walk is full of defects; stiffly projecting the leg, dragging after it the torso, the heel strikes the ground with a thud, jarring the spine.

There are almost as many walks as there are individuals. It is temperamental, as much an indicator of the habits, character and emotions, as the voice. One recognizes a friend by his step, even when heard but not seen. As we sit here, listen to a short lecture.

In our last lesson we considered the attitudes of the legs, and learned the emotional signification of each pose; we shall now find that each attitude is the basis of a walk.

Remembering that all the parts of the human body have a reciprocal action on one another, every step must be a nice adjustment of the opposition to be maintained between head, torso and limbs. The perfect walk must be straight, each step a foot apart (your own foot, not the ordinary foot-measure). Bobbing up and down, pitching, rolling, strutting, must be avoided as gymnastic crimes. The great work of the movement falls to the lot of the thigh, the vital division of the leg. This is the strongest portion of the frame.

An item I lately read illustrated this: In England, at country fairs, a man astonished bucolic audiences by his prowess in lifting a cannon weighing thousands of pounds. He supported it suspended from a belt around the hips. However, one fine day, a daring youth sought to emulate him, and, to his own astonishment, succeeded. "Come one, come all." Many more essayed, none failed; thus proving no extraordinary strength on the part of the showman, but more than ordinary wit in discovering the strength of the thigh. In modern athletic sports, the thigh does most of the hard work. The best rowing is from the hip, the arms serving to hold the oars.

To recapitulate what we have collected so far for our walk:

1. A straight forward step;

2. Harmonic poise;
3. Thigh-movement.

What is thigh-movement? Look! sweeping up Fifth avenue trots a thoroughbred; mark his action. With vital force he lifts his thigh, so to speak; lower leg and hoof hang loosely. The straightening of the knee plants the hoof. Now turn and observe me. I lift the thigh forward, lower leg and foot hang loosely; the unbending at my knee plants the foot, as simultaneously my weight sways on it.

And now, you ask, which should touch first, the ball or the heel of the foot? Strictly speaking, the ball, if we all were virtuous and restored the foot to the proportions of a bare foot; but, alas! the stern mandate of fashion decrees a heel on the shoe; so ordinary mortals must yield, and in planting the foot the heel will first touch mother earth. The bare foot is fashioned to grasp the ground. Carry the foot in transfer near the ground. High stepping is fine in sound, but neither horses nor men can afford it when either have work to do or races to run. The torso and head should sway in harmonic sympathy with every motion of the legs; this is the walk of animated attention, emotions that are vital.

Observe the processions of the Athenian youths and maidens on the Elgin marbles. In these processions, fantastic and involved, one finds each figure sculptured in marble action in various stages of this walk,—the normo-excentric. This is significant of a normo-vital poise of being; but, alas! as your eye roams over the passing crowd, we find no human example. That St. Bernard there comes toward us with majestic stride, fulfilling all the requirements. Man alone hops and halts, trudges and strides, limps and ambles. What says Byron?

> "Near this spot
> Are deposited the remains of one
> Who possessed beauty without vanity,
> Strength without insolence,
> Courage without ferocity,
> And all the virtues of man without his vices.
> This praise, which would be unmeaning flattery
> If inscribed over human ashes,
> Is but a just tribute to the memory of
> Boatswain, a dog."

Watch that restless crowd. Can you find me a human example? Appearing through the gleaming trees, with happy sun-kissed face, whistling an air from "Trovatore," comes a young Italian vender. On his head he balances a tray of plaster-casts, images of Venus, Mercury, Psyche. The necessity for perfect poise has been his task-master. Profit by the example; and, when you reach your home, practice the walk with a book on your head, walking straight on a chalked tape, the marks two feet apart (your own feet). Pin this tape in front of the looking-glass, and step on the marks as you see them reflected.

> "The perfection and power of the body as an instrument is manifested in three stages:
> 1. "Bodily power by practice;
> 2. "Bodily power by moral habit;
> 3. "Bodily power by immediate energy."—*Ruskin.*

So the walk may express your temperament (moral habit); it may express a passing emotion (immediate energy); or it may be gained by practice. Happy one if your temperament is the exciting cause of beautiful action. Hear Plato: "It is the testimony of the ancients that the madness which is of God is a nobler thing than the wisdom which is of men."

And again: "He who sets himself to any work with which the muses have to do without madness, thinking that by art alone he can do his work sufficiently, will be found vain and incapable; and the work of temperance and rationalism will be thrust aside and obscured by that of inspiration."

Very strong words, too strong, perhaps, for insertion here; and yet they emphasize what I wish you always to bear in mind. But do not mistake me; I am no advocate of the "inspiration of lazy mediocrity." I wish you only to remember "the supremacy of genius as the necessity of labor; for there never was, perhaps, a period in which so many and so vain efforts have been made to replace it by study and toil." Study and toil prepare a perfect mirror in which the vision of genius can be perfectly reflected; without it often the image comes torn and rent as from a broken glass.

The imagination, the ruling and divine power, is never governed. The rest of man is but an instrument on which that plays, a canvas on which that paints; harmoniously, if the strings be true, the canvas white and smooth; wildly, if one be broken, the other stained. Thus, you see, while work must be done, the instrument perfected, art is only valuable as it expresses goodness and greatness in the soul. Imitation may imitate the expression, but it can always be detected as imitation, and resembles truth as nearly as the cloud on a painted canvas is like one on heaven's canopy, flecked and thrilled with golden light.

"But the moment that inner part of man, or rather that entire and only being of the man of which cornea and retina, fingers and hands are all the mere servants and instruments, that manhood which has light in itself though the eyeball be sightless, and can gain in strength when the hand and the foot are hewn off and cast into the fire, the moment this part of the man stands forth with its solemn 'behold it is I,' then the work becomes art, indeed, perfect in honor, priceless in value, boundless in power."—*Ruskin.*

The tendency of the age is toward formulation of

science, not art. When we remember that within the last half century the real nature of earth, air, light, and of animal existence, was hardly dreamed of,—and that even now the mass of mankind fail to apprehend it, we realize what children we have been for more than six thousand years. A master of modern science says: "When men invented the locomotive, the child was learning to go; when they invented the telegraph, it was learning to speak." But the locomotive and the telegraph must be guided; and here a word of advice: When before the public in the pulpit, on the platform, or the stage, forget all rules, or rather make no effort to recall them. Your motto there should be heart-work, not head-work.

"Then why study art's rules and formulæ?" I hear you ask.

Because much of your practice will cling to you, without conscious thought; because nature rarely showers all her gifts on one head. Inspiration may be yours without bodily power to express; or you may be virtuosos without "the still small voice within." Rachel sought Samson for interpreter; she was virtuoso. Demosthenes and Talma were creators, but we all know their struggles to conquer the bodily powers in expression. So let us pray for "a quick, perceptive and eager heart, perfected by the intellect, and finally dealt with by the body under the direct guidance of these higher powers."

Are you rested? Shall we walk? Who comes toward us as we enter Fifth avenue? An actress, by her walk. Observe, she plants her foot with bent knee, using the knee as a spring. A soft, sinuous step, a panther-like effect. Very effective in its proper place, as expressive of controlled force, secrecy; we call that the normo-concentric walk. Imagine this scene in " Diplomacy: " Zicka is crossing the room to steal the letter in the casket. Words are unnecessary; her secret step betrays her errand. The difference between this walk and the first described, consists in the planting of the foot with bent knee; then, as the weight sways on it, the figure rises. No jar is possible to the frame, hence its selection by many actresses for grace. It is needless to add that it should be used only in portraying secret, sinuous character.

A walk taught by stage-managers, and selected by the society actor, is the excentro-concentric, expressing defiance. Observe me. I start in the defiant attitude, vital force flowing to toes before I move; rigid knee. I feel "how manly I am." Each advance step strikes the heel hard on the pavement, the torso dragged after. Behold, aptly to illustrate, stride two dudes. The windows in the opposite house almost jar as they pass.

"My knees sink under me; help or I die!" the despondent, despairing walk of prostration seems to exclaim.

Here toddles a wee one, hand in that of nurse. Baby, dear, you are toddling in the concentro-normal walk, expressing infancy or inferiority; very cunning in you, small atom, but quite out of place in Miss Flora McFlimsey. Watch her, as yonder she trots with soubrette steps. A little shake at the hips helps her legs to take their tiny pace. Miss Flora, you should sport cap and ribbons and muslin apron to be all in harmony.

Turn your head before Prof. Muggins is out of sight. With doubting step he hesitates and thinks; a slight pause, ever and anon; musing over protoplasm, professor?

An actor playing a blind part, asked my opinion of his performance.

"I have but one criticism to make," was my verdict. "Your legs are not blind."

"My legs blind! How can I make them so?"

I explained:

"Fearing to lose their equilibrium, the blind instinctively seek a broad base in standing and walking.

Each step is taken with rigid knee; the nor.-nor. attitude is the basis of this walk."

Also in vertigo and drunkenness, the sinking forces seek to recover their equilibrium on as broad a base as possible. It is the vulgar and peasant walk.

And now, attention to the turn. The concentro-excentric attitude is the one assumed in the change of direction. I throw my weight on the ball of the advanced foot, raising the heel and anchoring with the ball of the free foot; this leaves both heels free. So I turn to any point I choose; the free foot then points the changed direction. This saves numberless small steps, always awkward and especially so behind the footlights.

Central Park! A good arena for our race. Let us try a run. Here is a by-path, no one observing but those two black swans with crimson beaks, sailing majestically on that tree-encircled lake. Catch me, if you can. Ah! I outdistance you, for, like all women, you roll instead of run. Recall the attitude of the fighting gladiator, the excentro-excentric; forward leg strong, knee bent, torso thrown well forward. The run is a continuous succession of these attitudes. Try for me. Very well; you are an apt scholar. Shall we race again? We cannot; a gray-coated policeman appears. He eyes us with suspicion. He thinks us "children of too large a growth" for such games. We will go home; the sun is setting.

ÆSTHETIC GYMNASTICS.

Exercise I.—Back Fall.

(*a*) Assume attitude of prostration, con.-con. of legs; (*b*) sink as low as the back knee will allow; (*c*) then swing the body to the floor, striking the thigh of the back leg on one side just above the knee; (*d*) let torso fall back, simultaneously straightening bent knee. The entire body is now prone.

Exercise II.—Front Fall.

(*a*) Assume attitude of explosion, ex.-ex. of legs; (*b*) throw body forward, striking floor on thigh of strong leg. Be careful to protect the face with the forearms as you throw torso to the ground.

Exercise III.—Kneeling.

(*a*) Assume attitude of explosion, ex.-ex. of legs; (*b*) bend free leg until the knee rests on the ground.
N. B.—Always rest on knee which is toward the audience.

Exercise IV.—Bowing.

(*a*) Sink into attitude of prostration, con.-con. of legs; (*b*) rise slowly from it, carefully observing harmonic poise of head and torso in opposition to the legs.

N. B.—Sink on knee toward the audience. There are various degrees of bowing; the knee bends less in a slight obeisance.

Exercise V.—Sitting.

(*a*) Stand before a chair, attitude of legs con.-con.; right leg strong; (*b*) bend right knee as far down and out as is possible; (*c*) bend torso forward in opposition. The thigh now meets the chair and you are seated.

Exercise VI.—Rising from Sitting.

(*a*) Rise by bending torso forward and throwing weight on right leg; (*b*) when torso is raised from chair, throw weight on left leg, and (*c*) rise to nor.-ex. attitude of legs.

Exercise VII.—Rising from Back Fall.

(*a*) With the aid of the arm (right arm if the bent leg in falling was the right), raise the torso as you simultaneously bend under you the right leg; (*b*) throw yourself thus into a kneeling position, right knee touching the floor; (*c*) then rise as described below in the rise from kneeling.

Exercise VIII.—Rising from Front Fall.

This is about the same as rising from back fall. (*a*) The outstretched leg, say right, is bent under as the torso rises, aided to that rise by the right arm holding the weight for one instant, the palm on the floor; (*b*) from kneeling position, you then rise.

N. B.—The arm and knee which bear the weight should be on the same side.

Exercise IX.—*Rising from Kneeling.*

(*a*) Throw the weight on the free leg, *i. e.*, not the one the knee of which is on the ground; (*b*) rise from thence to attitude of legs nor.-ex.

N. B.—All of the foregoing stage business is in accordance with the system of Delsarte, which system is founded on the universal laws of equilibrium and grace. The three great things to be always borne in mind in every movement are ease, precision, harmony.

Exercise X.—*Pivoting.*

(*a*) Stand erect, both legs strong; (*b*) sway weight on to ball of right foot, heel clearing the ground, ball of left foot touching the ground; (*c*) turn toward left on the right ball, left ball following; (*d*) rest on heel of right foot. Your direction will then be toward the left. Reverse this to change the direction toward the right. Do not jar on the heel. (*e*) Stand in attitude nor.-ex.; (*f*) pivot on ball of advanced foot to attitude ex.-con. This completely reverses the attitude, the face replacing the back.

Exercise XI.—Rising on Toes.

(*a*) Stand in attitude con.-nor., heels together, toes diverging; (*b*) rise slowly on toes; sink as slowly. Be careful not to lurch back on heels and so jar the body. This develops the calves of the legs. The slowness with which you rise and sink in uninterrupted motion, is the chief merit of the foregoing exercise.

Dearest:

The clock struck one, your hour, but you came not; instead rat-tat-tat, a messenger, a telegram: "Am called away; will explain by letter;" and to-day your letter—such a blue one!—our chats and studies must cease for the present, unless I can teach by letter. I will send you concise summaries of the laws to be apprehended, the gymnastics to be essayed,—more I cannot promise. Inclosed find the lesson. Write me of your progress.

Your teacher and friend,

THE AUTHOR.

For articles on the Delsarte System of Dramatic Expression, elaborating the following, see *The Voice*, **Edgar S. Werner**, Publisher, No. 48 University Place, New York.

LESSON VI.

THE HAND.

We have to consider,—
1. The faces of the hand;
2. The functions of the hand;
3. The indications of the hand.

THE FACES OF THE HAND.

1. The palm, vital in nature, revelatory in expression;
2. The back, moral in nature, mystic in expression;
3. The side, mental in nature, indicative or definitive in expression.

THE FUNCTIONS OF THE HAND.

1. To define or indicate;
2. To affirm or deny;
3. To mold or detect;
4. To conceal or reveal;
5. To surrender or hold;
6. To accept or reject;

7. To inquire or acquire;
8. To support or protect;
9. To caress or assail.

Description of Movement.

1. (*a*) To define: first finger prominent; hand moves up and down, side to earth.

(*b*) To indicate: first finger prominent; hand points to object to be indicated.

2. (*a*) To affirm: hand, palm down, makes movement of affirmation up and down.

(*b*) To deny: hand, palm down, makes movement of negation from side to side.

3. (*a*) To mold: hand makes a movement as if molding a soft substance, as clay.

(*b*) To detect: rub the thumb across the fingers as if feeling a texture held between them. (A movement often made when following a train of thought.)

4. (*a*) To conceal: bring the palm of the hand toward you, the fingers at the same time gently closing on palm.

(*b*) To reveal: reverse the above movement, exposing palm.

5. (*a*) To surrender: closed hand opens, palm down, action as if dropping something on the ground.

(*b*) To hold: the hand closes as if to retain something.

6. (*a*) To accept: fingers close on upturned palm as if receiving something.

(*b*) To reject: fingers unclose from down-turned palm as if throwing something away.

7. (*a*) To inquire: a tremulous movement of the outstretched fingers as in the blind; palm down.

(*b*) To acquire: hand drawn toward you, fingers curve toward down-turned palm

8. (*a*) To support: palm up, making a flat surface as if supporting a weight.

(*b*) To protect: palm down; a movement of fingers as if covering what you protect.

9. (*a*) To caress: a movement of stroking up and down, or sideways. If sideways, one caresses the animal nature.

(*b*) To assail: palm down; the fingers make a convulsive movement of clutching.

THE INDICATIONS OF THE HAND.

1. The hand indicates the side of the being predominating in activity. This is shown by the point of departure of the gesture from its significant zone.

2. The hand indicates the condition of the being.

This is shown by the unfolding of the hand by itself, as illustrated in the attitudes of the hand.

3. The hand indicates the intention or attention of the being; this is shown by the inflections of the hand in gesture.

THE CONDITIONAL ATTITUDES OF THE HAND.

1.

Action: nor.-nor.

Signification: calm repose.

Description of action: hand normal.

That is, the thumb carried opposed to the second and third fingers. Test this by shutting the thumb on the two foregoing fingers; the first and little fingers are apart from these two. The thumb is the thermometer of will-power in the hand, as the palm is vital, the fingers mental. In the subdivision of the fingers, the first is mental, hence its predominance in defining; the little finger is expressive of the affections; the second and third together represent the vital tendencies. All we have to observe here is that in the normal attitude of the hand, its proper carriage is as follows:

1. Thumb exactly opposed to second and third fingers;

2. Second and third fingers touch each other;

3. Little and first fingers spread apart and a little back of their neighbors.

Hold this attitude lightly.

"Suppose I had asked the same service of three men, and that each had answered me with the single word 'yes,' accompanied by a gesture of the hand. If one of them had let his thumb approach the forefinger, it is plain to me that he would deceive me; for his thumb, thus placed, tells me that he is dead to my proposition.

"If I observe in the second a slight contraction of the thumb, I must believe that he, although indisposed to oblige me, will still do so from submission.

"But if the third oppose his thumb forcibly to the other fingers —— Oh! I can count on him; he will not deceive me. The abduction of his thumb tells me more in regard to his loyalty than all the assurances which he might give me."—*Delsarte.*

II.

Action: con.-nor.

Signification: indifference, prostration, imbecility, insensibility, or death.

Description of action: thumb attracted inward.

"I noticed, in fact, that in all these corpses the thumb displayed a similar tendency,—that of adduction or attraction inward.

"Now I prove that the thumbs of the dying man contracted at first in an almost imperceptible degree. * * * Thus, I had acquired the proof that not only does the adduction of the thumb characterize death, but that this phenomenon indicates the approach of death in proportion to its intensity."—*Delsarte.*

III.

Action: ex.-nor.

Signification: approbation, tenderness.

Description of action: the thumb abducted; the fingers curved gently.

"I noticed nurses who were distracted and indifferent to the children under their charge; in these, the thumb was invariably drawn toward the fingers, thus offering some resemblance to the contraction which it manifests in death. With other nurses, more affectionate, the fingers of the hand that held the child were visibly parted, displaying a thumb bent outward; but this eccentration rose to still more startling proportions in the mothers. There the thumb was bent violently as if to embrace a beloved being."—*Delsarte.*

IV.

Action: nor.-con.

Signification: calm self-possession, power.

Description of action: fold fingers on palm, thumb upright at side of first finger.

V.

Action: con.-con.

Signification: struggle, resolution, concentration of force.

Description of action: fold fingers on palm, thumb pressed tightly across the second joints of closed hand.

VI.

Action: ex.-con.

Signification: convulsion.

Description of action: fingers and thumb crooked toward centre of palm, hand nearly closed.

VII.

Action: nor.-ex.

Signification: animated attention or intention, earnestness.

Description of action: hand open, fingers straight, thumb spread.

VIII.

Action: con.-ex.

Signification: exasperation.

Description of action: hand as in convulsion, only more spread from palm; hand expanded, fingers crooked.

IX.

Action: ex.-ex.

Signification: exaltation of passion.

Description of action: hand spread to its greatest extent, fingers and thumb wide apart.

The attitudes of the hand color the voice, by the sympathy there is between the muscles and nerves of the hand and those of the throat and jaws.

Practice the line, —

"Shut the door!"

assuming by turn each attitude with both hands. Each attitude will effectually color the tone.

ÆSTHETIC GYMNASTICS.

Exercise I.

Raise arm in breadths; hand falling as if dead brings finger-tips level with shoulder. Arm still extended, sink wrist; arm stiff, recompose hand. This action brings hand from palm in to palm out, finger-tips raised. The level of finger-tips has not changed during the process.

Exercise II.

Sink wrist in every altitude; move the arm through the air, keeping hand as a dead weight. It will float as a feather.

N. B.—The foregoing must be practiced until easily performed.

SERPENTINE MOVEMENT.

Exercise III.

Sink wrist as previously explained; arm in breadths. Rotate wrist until fingers point to ground, palm out. Raise hand on wrist, palm in. Elbow has been stiff. Now, bend elbow until finger-tips touch shoulder, simultaneously sinking upper arm to side of torso. Without unbending, raise elbow up and out; wrist remains level with armpit, hand falls decomposed. Now, sink elbow again to side; combine last with a rotary inward movement of upper arm, which throws decomposed hand palm out and down. Straighten elbow; this will throw the hand out and up. Recompose hand.

N. B.—It is difficult to write out movement, which needs the living teacher. The above must be done with great accuracy or it is worthless.

CHART III.
Conditional Attitudes of the Hand.

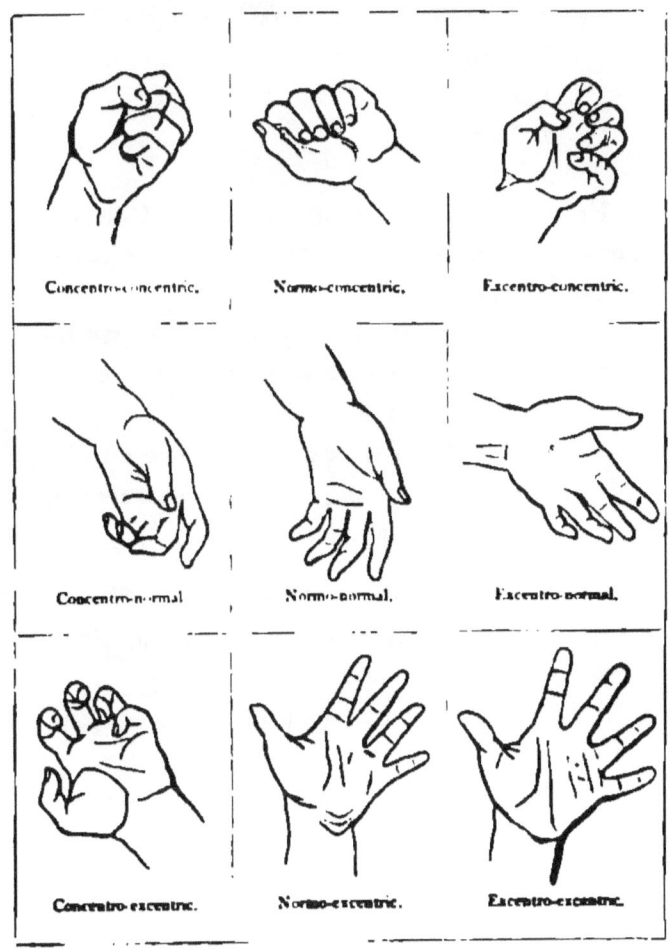

LESSON VII.

THE HAND.—Continued.

THE POSITIONS OF THE HAND IN SPACE, RELATIVE TO THE CENTRES OF GRAVITY AND BEING.

Man is *en rapport* with :
1. Nature;
2. Humanity;
3. Divinity.

He has radiations to each. Nature and divinity are the two extremes; the centre of gravity *down*, the universal centre *up*.

The human radiations between man and man are in the lengths. The individual centre is represented by the torso, which figures the love of the being. Thus man stands on the earth, communicates with his fellow-beings expanding from individual centres, and looks upward to the universal.

THE RELATIVE ATTITUDES OF THE HAND.

1. Nor.-nor. Hand straight with forearm, side to earth.
2. Con.-nor. Hand straight with forearm, palm turned to earth.

3. Ex.-nor. Hand straight with forearm, palm turned up from earth.
4. Nor.-con. Palm turned to self, side to earth.
5. Con.-con. Palm in, fingers turned to earth.
6. Ex.-con. Palm in, fingers up from earth.
7. Nor.-ex. Palm out, side to earth.
8. Con.-ex. Palm out, fingers to earth.
9. Ex.-ex. Palm out, fingers from earth.

THE INFLECTIONS OF THE HAND.

The abbreviations used below describe the relative *attitudes* of the hand. For their explanation, refer to the foregoing definitions.

1. Hand nor.-nor., moves up and down; signifies simple statement, formulation, or definition.

2. Hand con.-nor., moves from side to side; signifies impatient negation.

3. Hand ex.-nor., moves from side to side; signifies distribution.

4. Hand from ex.-con. to con.-ex., signifies salutation.

5. Hand from con.-ex. to ex.-con., signifies appellation.

6. Hand from ex.-ex. to con.-con., signifies grasping, lust, assailment; curved fingers.

7. Hand from con.-con. to ex.-ex., signifies exaltation, surprise.

8. Hand from nor.-con. to nor.-ex., signifies exposition, revelation.

9. Hand from nor.-ex. to nor.-con., signifies concealment, mysticism, deceit.

ÆSTHETIC GYMNASTICS.

Exercise I.

Bend torso forward at waist; simultaneously raise arms back in opposition.

Exercise II.

Bend torso backward at waist; simultaneously raise arms forward in opposition.

Exercise III.

Raise arms slowly over head, commencing at shoulder level. At the same time head must sink on breast in opposition.

Exercise IV.

Let arms fall, head rising in opposition.

Exercise V.

Sway arms to the right, head turning to the left in opposition.

Exercise VI.

Sway arms to the left, head turning to the right in opposition.

GLADIATOR OPPOSITIONS.

Exercise VII.

Take attitude ex.-ex. of legs, signifying explosion; right leg strong. Simultaneously raise left arm in front, right arm back. Return to attitude con.-nor. of legs, heels together. Arms drop to side.

Exercise VIII.

Take attitude ex.-ex. of legs; left leg strong. Right arm raised in front simultaneously with left arm back. Return to attitude con.-nor. of legs. Arms drop to side.

Repeat the above movements a number of times in quick succession.

The arm in excentric gesture, *i. e.*, gesture in the lengths, should always be in opposition to the forward leg to maintain perfect equilibrium.

LESSON VIII.

THE HAND.—Continued.

THE AFFIRMATIONS OF THE HAND.

There are many affirmations of the hand. Below are nine. The abbreviations, nor.-nor., etc., describe the relative *attitudes* of the hand.

An affirmation is a movement up and down.

1. Hand nor.-nor.

Signification: Teacher's affirmation. It defines.

2. Hand con.-nor.

Signification: Patron's affirmation. It protects.

3. Hand ex.-nor.

Signification: Champion's affirmation. It supports.

4. Hand nor.-con.

Signification: Conservative's affirmation. It limits.

5. Hand con.-con.

Signification: Tyrant's affirmation. It commands.

6. Hand ex.-con.

Signification: Seer's affirmation. It mystifies.

7. Hand nor.-ex.

Signification: Saint's affirmation. It reveals.

8. Hand con.-ex.

Signification: Bigot's affirmation. It rejects all opposed.

9. Hand ex.-ex.

Signification: Orator's affirmation. It paints, demonstrates or protests.

The hand supplements the expression of the face.

The two hands clasped in the various conditional attitudes, as power, struggle, convulsion, etc., does not change the meaning.

ÆSTHETIC GYMNASTICS.
THE COMMAND "GO."

This movement takes place in the lengths.

Exercise I.

Raise arm in front level with the shoulder. Rotate hand into ex.-nor. relative position, first finger indicating object.

Exercise II.

Withdraw arm; elbow bends without changing the altitude. When wrist is level with armpit, raise elbow; hand falls decomposed. Sink elbow; unbend it; upper arm has continued a backward sweep during preceding movement. Altitude of first finger unchanged.

Exercise III.

The arm, stretched to its full length, is now behind, level with shoulder. Sink wrist until hand shall be level with arm, palm down, first finger pointing as if to an exit.

Exercise IV.

Practice evolution of muscular action in gesture of arms thus:
1. Shoulder;
2. Upper arm;
3. Elbow;
4. Forearm;
5. Wrist;
6. Hand.

Exercise V.

Practice involution from action to repose thus:
1. Hand;
2. Wrist;
3. Forearm;
4. Elbow;
5. Upper arm;
6. Shoulder.

Exercise VI.

Practice arm-movements in evolution-motion, raising the arm in every degree of altitude.

Notice that the forearm forms a more and more acute angle with the upper arm as the altitude rises. Begin the unbending of the forearm before the upper arm reaches the destined level, so the hand recomposes as the upper arm ceases motion.

N. B.—I cannot too strongly call your attention to this exercise.

The law of evolution is also exemplified in the perfect walk.

Practice involution of body thus:

Exercise VII.

Bow head as you raise hand; then torso as you bend forearm toward the breast.

Practice evolution of body thus:

Exercise VIII.

Raise torso as you unbend forearm; then head as you expand hand.

LESSON IX.

THE ARM.

There are three things to be noted in order to fully understand the motions of the arm:

1. The articulations;
2. The attitudes;
3. The inflections.

The articulations of the arm are three:

1. The shoulder, which is the thermometer of sensibility and passion;
2. The elbow, which is the thermometer of the affections and self-will;
3. The wrist, which is the thermometer of vital energy.

THE SHOULDER.

"The shoulder, in every man who is moved or agitated, rises sensibly, his will playing no part in the ascension; the developments of this involuntary act are in absolute relation of proportion to the passional intensity whose numeric measure they form. The shoulder may, therefore, be fitly called *the thermometer of sensibility.*"—*Delsarte.*

1. The shoulder raised indicates sensibility, passion;
2. The shoulder dropped indicates prostration, insensibility, death;

3. The shoulder advanced indicates endurance, patience.

THE ELBOW.

"Three centres in the arm: The shoulder, for pathetic action; the elbow, which approaches the body by reason of humility, and reciprocally, that is, inversely, for pride; lastly, the hand, for fine, spiritual and delicate actions."—*Delsarte.*

1. The elbow turned out indicates tenderness, force, audacity, self-assertion, conceit;
2. The elbow turned in indicates suppression of self, poverty of spirit, weakness, imbecility;
3. The elbow normal indicates calm repose, modesty, unconsciousness of self.

THE WRIST.

1. The wrist turned out demonstrates vital energy in action;
2. The wrist turned in demonstrates vital energy in accumulation, concealment, concentration;
3. The wrist normal demonstrates vital energy in repose, calm.

ÆSTHETIC GYMNASTICS.

SPIRAL MOVEMENT.

This movement takes place in the heights and depths.

N. B.—Keep in mind evolution of motion.

The Arm.

Exercise.

(*a*) Bring arm directly in front of body, muscular force acting only in upper arm. A rotary movement of the arm has turned the eye of the elbow (commonly called crazy-bone) to the front. Now follows the evolution of motion. (*b*) Putting force in upper arm, raise it to level of shoulder in front. The forearm and hand must hang decomposed. (*c*) At level of shoulder, force flows into forearm and unbends it; upper arm still rising. When arm is straight, (*d*) a rotary movement of wrist turns hand; (*e*) force flows into hand, raising it on line with arm, palm in. The arm is now directly over head, fingers pointing up.

This exercise consists in evolution of motion carried to the altitude of absolute truth.

LESSON X.

THE ARM.—Continued.

THE ATTITUDES OF THE ARM.

I.

Action: nor.-nor.

Signification: suspense of will in its attention or intention.

Description of action: elbows bent and pressed to sides brings wrists to level of chest. Hands fall decomposed.

II.

Action: con.-nor.

Signification: calm resignation of will.

Description of action: arms crossed on breast.

III.

Action: ex.-nor.

Signification: expansion of will-power in the assertion of its force, or affection.

Description of action: arms extended from shoulders in breadths; elbows unbent.

IV.

Action: nor.-con.

Signification: calm repose, indifference.

Description of action: arms hanging from shoulders at sides.

V.

Action: con.-con.

Signification: subjective reflection, force in ambush (*i. e.*, force concealed).

Description of action: arms hang back of body.

VI.

Action: ex.-con.

Signification: objective reflection, force in preparation.

Description of action: arms hang full length in front of body.

VII.

Action: nor.-ex.

Signification: vital repose, self-assertion, insolence, defiance.

Description of action: elbows bent, hands on hips; eye of elbow toward front.

VIII.

Action: con.-ex.

Signification: vital concentration, suppressed passion, reflective form of excitement or vitality.

Description of action: arms folded tightly on chest; forearms are nearly level with shoulders.

IX.

Action: ex.-ex.

Signification: exaltation, passional explosion.

Description of action: arms extended their full length in front, level with shoulders.

ÆSTHETIC GYMNASTICS.

Exercise.

(a) With both arms, execute the spiral movement to the altitude of absolute truth; both arms are now over the head; *(b)* decompose hands, then forearms; *(c)* sweep upper arms into breadths; *(d)* unbend elbows; *(e)* expand hands. The arms finish in attitude ex.-nor., signifying expansion of will in force, or tenderness.

One arm should slightly precede the action of the other.

LESSON XI.

THE ARM.—Continued.

THE INFLECTIONS OF THE ARM.

I.

Action: nor.-nor.

Signification: declaration.

Description of action: movement of arm directly in breadths; hand nor.-nor.; relative.

II.

Action: con.-nor.

Signification: negation.

Description of action: movement of arm in breadths; hand con.-nor.; relative.

III.

Action: ex.-nor.

Signification: rejection.

Description of action: oblique movement of arm; hand ex.-ex.; relative.

IV.

Action: nor.-con.

Signification: caress.

Description of action: movement of arm in heights and depths; hand nor.-nor.; relative; animal caress in breadths; hand con.-nor.; relative.

V.

Action: con.-con.

Signification: affirmation.

Description of action: movement of arm in heights and depths; hand con.-nor.; relative.

VI.

Action: ex.-con.

Signification: appellation.

Description of action: movement of arm from depths to heights; hand ex.-nor.; relative.

VII.

Action: nor.-ex.

Signification: acceptation.

Description of action: movement of arm in lengths; hand ex.-nor.; relative.

VIII.

Action: con.-ex.

Signification: attraction.

Description of action: movement of arm in lengths toward torso; hand ex.-ex.; relative.

IX.

Action: ex.-ex.

Signification: repulsion.

Description of action: movement from torso of arm in lengths; hand ex.-ex.; relative.

ÆSTHETIC GYMNASTICS.
PRIMARY OPPOSITIONS OF THE ARM AND HEAD.

Exercise I.—Mental or Normal Calm of Being.

Take position of legs con.-ex., weight on right foot; head and arm quiet.

Exercise II.—Resigned Appeal to Heaven.

(a) Right shoulder rises slightly, while head sinks in opposition; *(b)* upper arm makes rotary movement, which turns eye of elbow out; *(c)* then forearm unbends; *(d)* hand expands in tenderness; head has been slowly rising in opposition and is right, oblique, back, when movement ceases.

Exercise III.—Accusation.

(a) Upper-arm muscles swing arm to attitude ex.-ex.; *(b)* rotate wrist; *(c)* expand hand into ex.-nor.; relative. (Head has sunk in opposition to level position.)

Exercise IV.—Imprecation.

(a) Swing arm above head; *(b)* expand hand ex.-ex., relative, and con.-ex., conditional, expressing execration. (Head has sunk as low as possible, thrusting out chin.)

Exercise V.—Remorse.

Hand decomposes, then forearm; this drops hand on back of head, which has risen in opposition to meet it; eye of elbow to front.

Exercise VI.—Deep Thought, Grief or Shame.

Head and arm do not separate, but, united, sink on chest.

Exercise VII.—Reproach.

(*a*) Head and arm separate; (*b*) head rises and rotates to the right, while (*c*) hand and forearm decomposing, drops hand near left armpit and forearm across chest.

Exercise VIII.—Repulsion from Affection.

(*a*) Upper-arm muscles swing arm into breadths; (*b*) forearm unbends; (*c*) hand expands, back of hand to front; (*d*) head rotates in opposition to left.

Exercise IX.—Pathetic Protest or Benediction.

(*a*) Upper-arm muscles swing arm to attitude ex.-ex.; (*b*) hand expands, con.-nor., signifying benediction. Expanding ex.-ex., it expresses pathetic appeal or protest.

N. B.—The action of head and arm in above movements must be made simultaneously. Each action flows into the subsequent one. Always retain a gesture as long as the same thought or emotion is retained, or one remains in the same mood.

"External gesture being only the reverberation of interior gesture, which gives it birth and rules it, should be its inferior in development.

"Nothing is more deplorable than a gesture without a motive."
—*Delsarte.*

Moral Division.

LESSON XII.

THE TORSO.

There are three things to be known in relation to the torso:
1. Its significant zones;
2. Its attitudes;
3. Its inflections.

Its zones we have already studied, but will here recapitulate.

ZONES OF THE TORSO.

Mental Zone: The seat of conscience, honor, manhood and womanhood.

Moral Zone: Seat of the affections.

Vital Zone: Seat of the appetites.

The zones of the torso are the points of departure or arrival for a gesture. As such they indicate the side of the being predominating in expression.

In emotion, if the gesture seeks the chest, self-respect predominates; for that is the mental zone.

If the gesture seeks the heart-region, the affections predominate; for that is the moral zone.

If the gesture seeks the abdomen, the appetites predominate; for that is the vital zone.

In the carriage of the torso, the prominent zone is very significant of the being.

Above all things, protruding the abdomen should be avoided; the best carriage throws the moral zone into prominence.

ATTITUDES OF THE TORSO.

The torso has two species of attitudes:

1. Conditional attitudes; that is, those produced by the physical condition of the torso in itself;
2. Relative attitudes; that is, those relating the torso to the object in nature, or to the image in mind.

The conditional attitudes of the torso are three:

1. Expansion; indicating different degrees of excitement, vehemence, and power in the will;
2. Contraction; indicating different degrees of timidity, effort, pain, or convulsion of will;
3. Relaxation; indicating different degrees of surrender, indolence, intoxication, prostration, or insensibility in the will.

Relative Attitudes.

The torso is endowed with three forms of expression in its variable movements:

1. Bearings;

2. Attitudes;

3. Inflections.

Its bearings and attitudes are the most deeply expressive.

Its inflections are all indicative of weakness, real or assumed.

The torso represents the moral element, or love of the being. It is the weight and centre of the body, as love is the weight and centre of the being. It is the core, so to speak, of the man.

The relative attitudes of the torso are three:

1. Leaning *to* the object. If the attitude is direct, the attraction is vital or objective; if the attitude is oblique, the attraction is moral or subjective;

2. Leaning *from* the object, if direct, signifies vital or objective repulsion; if the attitude is oblique, moral or subjective repulsion;

3. Leaning *before* the object denotes vital or objective humility, shame or obsequiousness; if oblique, moral or subjective humility, shame or reverence.

INFLECTIONS OF THE TORSO.

1. Up and down indicates the despair of the weak; oscillation of the will alternately excited and depressed;

2. From side to side indicates carelessness; vacil-

lation of the will; indifference to the equilibrium of the will;

3. Twisting or rotary movement indicates childish impatience; spasmodic convulsion of the will; chaos of the will.

ÆSTHETIC GYMNASTICS.

The primary inflections of gesture comprise three types of motion; they are usually united. We name them direct, circular, and oblique inflections.

The flexor movements are direct; the rotary movements circular; the abductory movements oblique.

Study the following chart, and mark well the direction of the arrowheads. They apply to the right arm and hand. The inside quarter circles, drawn concave in relation to the outer circle, should be followed by the right hand or arm as they are curved.

CHART IV.

Movements of Right Arm and Hand.

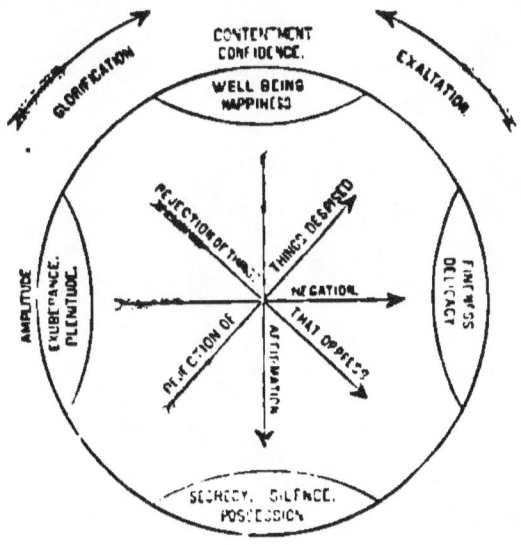

Mental Division.

LESSON XIII.

THE HEAD.

There are three things to be known in relation to the head:

1. Its significant zones;
2. Its attitudes;
3. Its inflections.

The zones of the head we have already studied as points of departure or arrival for the gesture. However, to recapitulate:

The zones of the face are three.

1. Forehead and eye are mental;
2. Nose and cheek are moral;
3. Mouth and chin are vital.

The top and back of the head also divide into three zones:

1. The zone above the forehead is mental;
2. The zone on top of the head is moral;
3. The zone at the back of the head is vital.

In emotion, if the hand seeks the chin, vital instincts predominate: namely, appetites, passions;

While if the hand seeks the forehead, the mental instincts predominate;

If the hand touches the cheeks, the moral instincts; that is, the affections, predominate.

CHART V.

ZONES OF THE HEAD.

1. Vital.
2. Mental.
3. Moral.

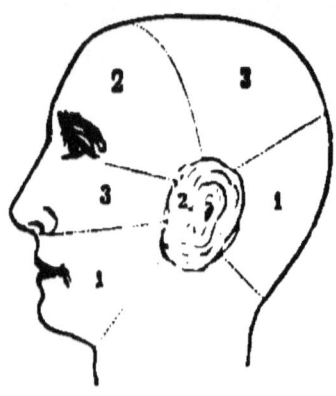

ATTITUDES OF THE HEAD.

I.

Action: nor.-nor.

Signification: calm repose, or indifference.

Description of action: head level between the shoulders, inclined neither to right nor left, up nor down.

II.

Action: con.-nor.

Signification: trust, tenderness, sympathy, affection, esteem from the soul.

Description of action: head leans toward object, but must not be raised, depressed or rotated.

III.

Action: ex.-nor.

Signification: distrust, esteem from the senses.

Description of action: head leans from object, but must not be raised, depressed or rotated.

IV.

Action: nor.-con.

Signification: reflection, concentration, scrutiny, humility.

Description of action: head sinks on chest midway between the shoulders.

THE HEAD.   133

V.

Action: con.-con.

Signification: humility plus trust and affection = veneration, adoration.

Description of action: head depressed and toward object; not rotated.

VI.

Action: ex.-con.

Signification: scrutiny plus distrust = suspicion, hate, envy, jealousy.

Description of action: head depressed and from object; not rotated.

VII.

Action: nor.-ex.

Signification: exaltation, explosion from self as a centre, a lifting to the universal.

Description of action: head thrown back midway between the shoulders.

VIII.

Action: con.-ex.

Signification: exaltation plus trust, abandonment plus trust = resignation or abandonment to sense or soul.

Description of action: head thrown back and toward object.

IX.

Action: ex.-ex.

Signification: exaltation plus self-assertion or distrust = arrogance.

Description of action: head thrown back and from object.

Inflections of the head, other than those necessary for opposition of movement, should be avoided as weak. Two are in common use: (1) A rotation from shoulder to shoulder, expressing negation; and (2) a movement down, signifying assent.

ÆSTHETIC GYMNASTICS.
Exercise.

Practice the nine attitudes of the head. Then rotate the head in each attitude, taking care not to change the significant angle of the head in relation to the shoulders.

N. B.—The arrangement of Charts VI and VIII is different from the other Charts in order that the Plane of the Superior may be at the top and the Plane of the Inferior at the bottom. The philosophical harmony is not thereby disturbed.

CHART VI.

ATTITUDES OF THE HEAD.
PLANE OF THE SUPERIOR.

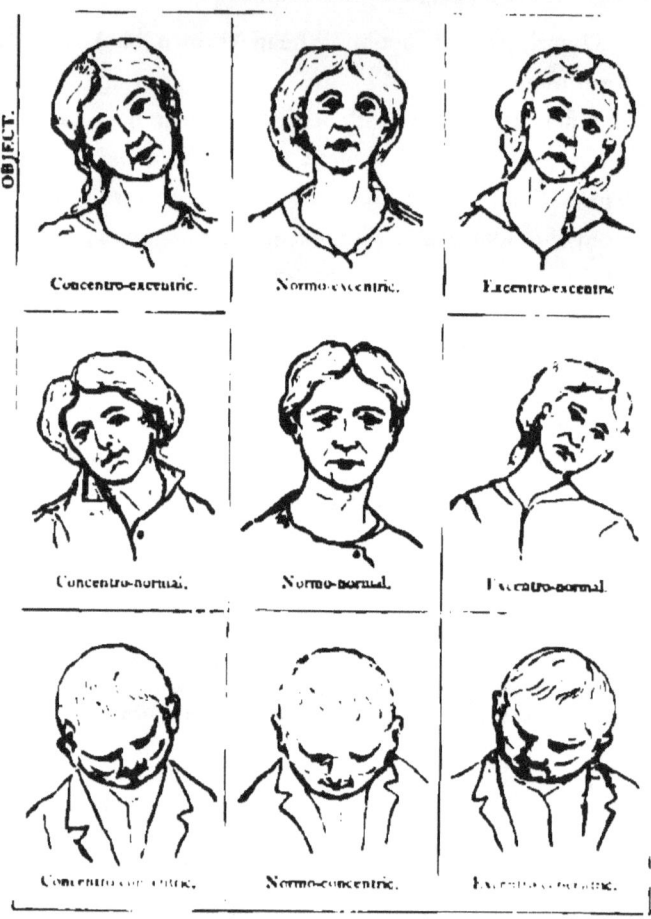

PLANE OF THE INFERIOR.

CHART VII.

Divisions of the Head.

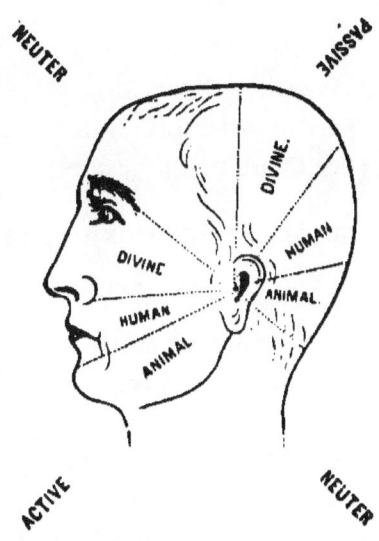

LESSON XIV.

THE HEAD—Continued.

The head is divided into three divisions:
1. Active;
2. Passive;
3. Neuter.

The active division of the head has three parts:
1. Divine;
2. Human;
3. Animal.

The passive division is divided in the same manner. (See Chart VII, page 136.)

THE ACTIVE DIVISION OF THE HEAD.

THE EYES.

There are two sets of agents in the eye:
1. Passive, which is organized *in* the eyeball;
2. Active, which is organized *about* the eyeball.

The eyeball is simply an indicator of the direction from which an impression comes, or to which an expression goes. Its significance arises from the relation it indicates between the subject and the object.

Pupil is mental;
White is vital;
Iris is moral.

Man has more white in the eye than any other animal, showing more life in the mind than any other animal.

SIGNIFICATION AND ACTION OF THE EYEBALL.

I.

Action: nor.-nor.

Signification: neutral.

Description of action: eyeball is calm midway between the two corners.

II.

Action: con.-nor.

Signification: simple mystic regard of object or thing.

Description of action: eye is turned *to* object, neither raised nor depressed.

III.

Action: ex.-nor.

Signification: simple mystic attention to subject or idea.

Description of action: eye is turned *from* object, neither raised nor depressed.

IV.

Action: nor.-con.

Signification: simple subjection of image, object or idea to self.

Description of action: eye is depressed midway between the two corners.

V.

Action: con.-con.

Signification: exaltation of self in mystic regard of object.

Description of action: eye is depressed and turned *to* object.

VI.

Action: ex.-con.

Signification: exaltation of self in mystic attention to subject or idea.

Description of action: eye is depressed and turned *from* object.

VII.

Action: nor.-ex.

Signification: simple subjection of self to object, image or idea.

Description of action: eye is raised midway between the two corners.

VIII.

Action: con.-ex.

Signification: subjection of self in mystic regard of object.

Description of action: eye is raised and turned *to* object.

IX.

Action: ex.-ex.

Signification: subjection of self in mystic attention to subject or idea.

Description of action: eye is raised and turned *from* object.

Beside the foregoing, there is a converging, a diverging, and a parallel gaze of the eye.

The converging is the ordinary gaze;

The diverging is the gaze of vertigo, drunkenness, insanity;

The parallel, having no appreciable focus, is the gaze of ecstacy. The mind seems to be viewing an object which the eye cannot focus.

ÆSTHETIC GYMNASTICS.

Exercise I.

Using a hand-glass, take nor.-nor. eye; keeping eyeball steady, raise lid as high as possible above iris.

Exercise II.

Keeping lid raised and steady, move the eyeball into all the attitudes of the chart. (See Chart VIII, page 142.)

N. B.— This exercise accustoms lid and eyeball to separate and independent action, and should be practiced until easy to accomplish.

CHART VIII.

Attitudes of the Eyeball.

PLANE OF THE SUPERIOR.

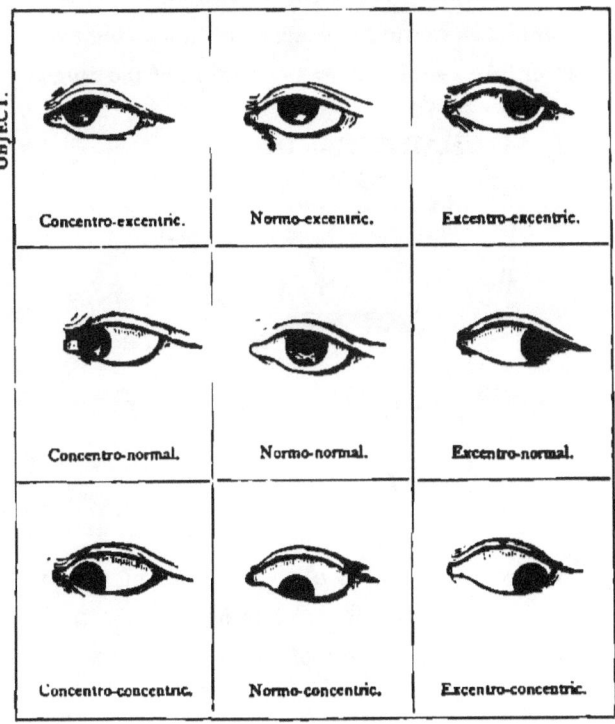

PLANE OF THE INFERIOR.

N. B.—Plane of the superior indicates the upraising of the eyeball. Plane of the Inferior the depressing of the eyeball.

To object—the eyeball turned to the object. From object, vice versa.

LESSON XV.

ACTIVE AGENTS OF THE EYE.

Brow—Upper Lid—Under Lid.

Brow = mental; reveals condition of the *mind;*
Upper lid = moral; reveals condition of the *will;*
Lower lid = vital; reveals condition of the *senses.*

CHART IX.—THE BROW.

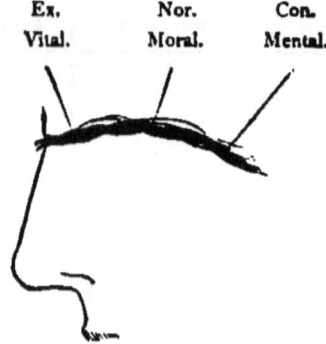

1. Ex. (near the nose); vital force of mind;
2. Con.; mental force of mind;
3. Nor.; moral force of mind.

SIGNIFICATION AND ACTION OF THE EYEBROW.

I.

Action: nor.-nor.

Signification: calm serenity of mind; vital and mental force inactive.

Description of action: brow normal.

II.

Action: con.-nor.

Signification: calm reflection; vital force concentrated; mental force full, but serene.

Description of action: ex. of brow depressed.

III.

Action: ex.-nor.

Signification: anxiety, calm suffering; vital force exalted, mental force quiet.

Description of action: ex. of brow raised.

IV.

Action: nor.-con.

Signification: timid or sterile mind; vital force in repose, mental force dormant and depressed.

Description of action: con. of brow lowered.

V.

Action: con.-con.

Signification: timid reflection; vital force concentrated, mental force prostrated.

Description of action: ex. and con. of brow lowered.

VI.

Action: ex.-con.

Signification: pain, agony, mental despair; vital force exalted, mental force prostrated, depressed.

Description of action: ex. of brow raised; con. of brow depressed.

VII.

Action: nor.-ex.

Signification: passional excitement of mind, imagination; vital force quiet, mental force exalted.

Description of action: con. of brow raised.

VIII.

Action: con.-ex.

Signification: fury, madness; vital force concentrated, mental force exalted.

Description of action: ex. of brow lowered; con. of brow raised.

IX.

Action: ex.-ex.

Signification: painful passion, terror, fear; vital and mental force exalted.

Description of action: ex. and con. of brow raised.

UPPER EYELID.

I.

Action: nor.-nor.

Signification: calm attention or intention.

Description of action: edge of lid half-way between pupil and top of iris.

II.

Action: con.-nor.

Signification: indifference to object; tendency to subject in mind; rejection of object by will.

Description of action: lid falls to top of pupil.

III.

Action: ex.-nor.

Signification: animated attention or intention.

Description of action: lid touches top of iris.

IV.

Action: nor.-con.

Signification: intense consideration of subject within.

Description of action: lid falls half-way between pupil and bottom of iris.

V.

Action: con.-con.

Signification: prostration, sleep, insensibility or death.

Description of action: lid is completely shut.

VI.

Action: ex.-con.

Signification: subjectivity or interiority of mind.

Description of action: lid half covers pupil.

VII.

Action: nor.-ex.

Signification: exaltation.

Description of action: lid raised, showing line of white above iris.

VIII.

Action: con.-ex.

Signification: passional tendency.

Description of action: lid shows a slight line of white above iris, less than in nor.-ex.

IX.

Action: ex.-ex.

Signification: madness.

Description of action: lid raised to its highest point above iris.

LOWER EYELID.

Lower lid normal = calm;
Lower lid raised = sensitiveness;
Lower lid depressed = death.

Inner corner near nose when raised denotes sensitiveness to pain;

Outer corner raised denotes sensitiveness to pleasure.

SIMPLE COMBINATIONS OF BROW AND UPPER LID.

By combining the nine positions of the brow with the nine positions of the upper lid, you can form eighty-one combinations.

Nine of these are described below. (See Chart X, page 152; for a second nine see Chart XI, page 153.)

I.

Action: nor.-nor.
Signification: calm serenity.
Description of action: brow normal = nor.; lid normal = nor.

II.

Action: con.-nor.

Signification: calm reflection, concentrated attention or intention, with calm of will.

Description of action: brow depressed = con.; lid normal = nor.

III.

Action: ex.-nor.

Signification: calm indifference.

Description of action: brow raised = ex.; lid normal = nor.

IV.

Action: nor.-con.

Signification: subjective reflection, interiority of will, quiescent tendency of will in mind.

Description of action: brow normal = nor.; lid depressed = con.

V.

Action: con.-con.

Signification: deep thought, subjective action of mind.

Description of action: brow depressed = con.; lid depressed = con.

VI.

Action: ex.-con.

Signification: mental contempt, supercilious regard.

Description of action: brow raised = ex.; lid depressed = con.

VII.

Action: nor.-ex.

Signification: eagerness to know plus inability to mentally solve = stupor.

Description of action: brow calm = nor.; lid raised = ex.

VIII.

Action: con.-ex.

Signification: resolution, concentrated eagerness of will.

Description of action: brow depressed = con.; lid raised = ex.

IX.

Action: ex.-ex.

Signification: surprise.

Description of action: brow raised = ex.; lid raised = ex.

N. B.—In the abbreviations above used, the last term signifies the position of the lid; the first, that of the brow.

ÆSTHETIC GYMNASTICS.

Exercise I.

Practice the combinations of brow and lid. (See Chart X, page 152, and Chart XI, page 153.)

Exercise II.

Before a mirror, concentrate your attention on con. of brow; try to raise and depress it, other parts of the brow remaining quiet.

CHART X.

Simple Combinations of Upper Lid and Brow.

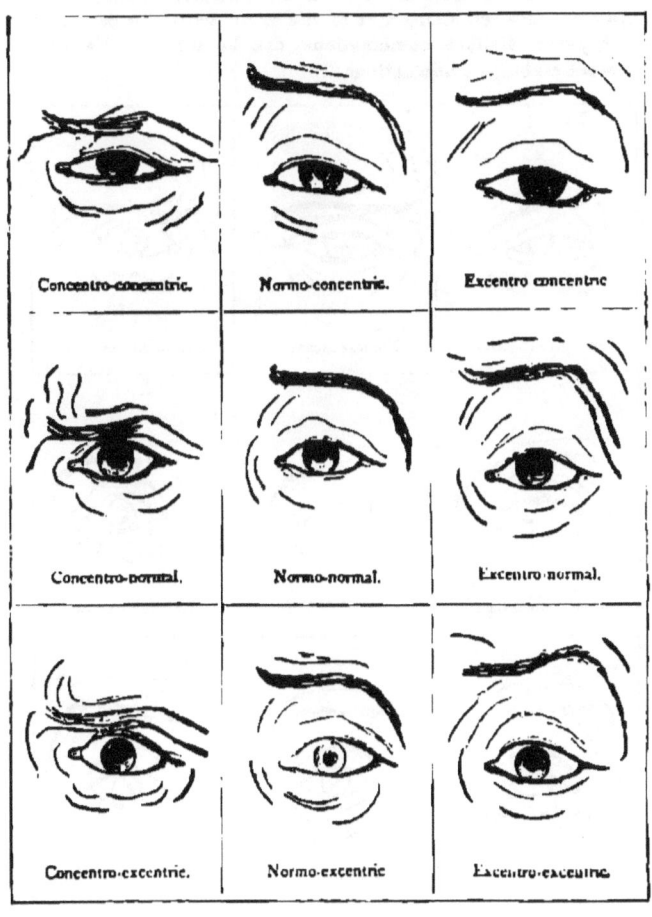

CHART XI.

COMBINATIONS OF UPPER LID AND BROW.

N. B.—In this chart the brow is the final term, the upper lid the first. By combining nine of the brow with nine of the lid eighty-one distinct combinations can be made. We here present eighteen combinations.

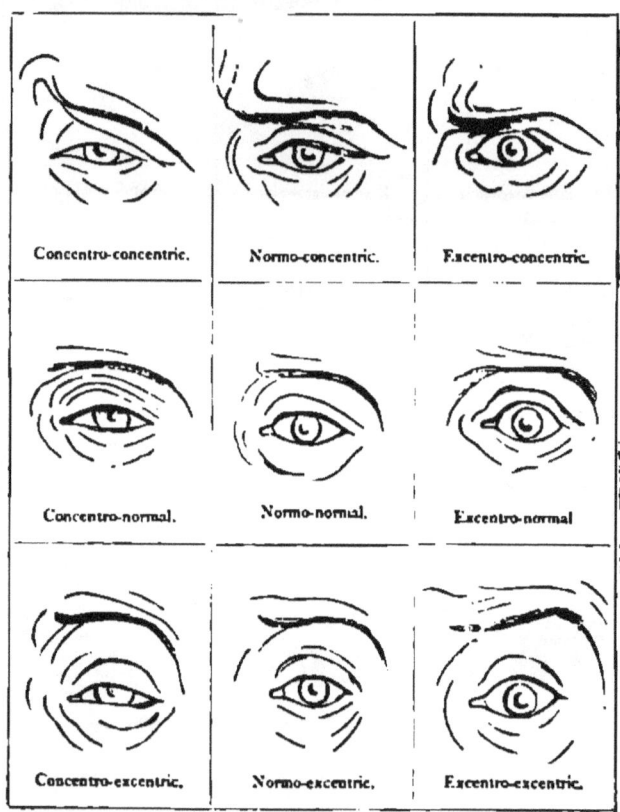

CHART XII.

Expressions of the Eyebrow.

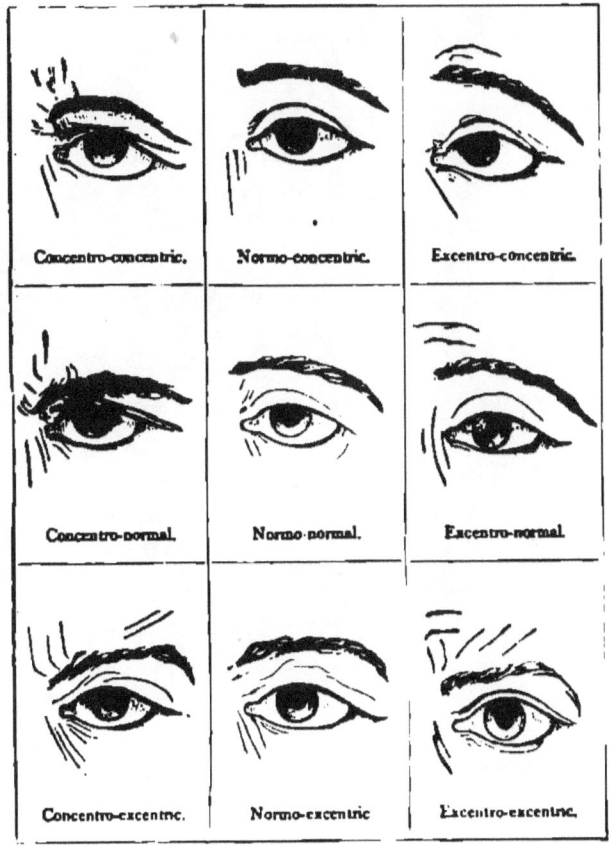

LESSON XVI.

PROFILES.

There are three primitive and characteristic profiles:

1. STRAIGHT.

2. CONCAVE.

3. CONVEX.

The straight profile is the best;
The concave is cold, chaste;
The convex is warm, sensual.

As each feature may be straight, concave or convex, a combination of the lines produces many and varied profiles.

The form of each feature is either congenital, or stamped from long habit.

EXPRESSIONS OF THE NOSE.

I.
Action: nor.-nor.
Signification: calm serenity, indifference.
Description of action: nostrils in repose.

II.
Action: con.-nor.
Signification: insensibility, hardness, cruelty.
Description of action: nostrils contracted.

III.
Action: ex.-nor.
Signification: sensibility, excitement, passion.
Description of action: nostrils dilated.

IV.
Action: nor.-con.
Signification: aggression.

Description of action: nose wrinkled laterally between eyebrows.

V.
Action: con.-con.
Signification: aggression plus cruelty = hate.
Description of action: nostrils contracted; nose wrinkled between eyebrows.

VI.
Action: ex.-con.
Signification: aggression plus scorn = fury.
Description of action: nostrils dilated; nose wrinkled between eyebrows.

VII.
Action: nor.-ex.
Signification: sensuousness, lasciviousness.
Description of action: nostrils raised.

VIII.
Action: con.-ex.
Signification: sensuousness plus insensibility or rejection = contempt.
Description of action: nostrils contracted and raised.

IX.

Action: ex.-ex.

Signification: sensuousness plus excitement = scorn.

Description of action: nostrils dilated and raised.

ÆSTHETIC GYMNASTICS.

Exercise.

Dilate and contract the nostrils as rapidly as possible; move no other portion of the face.

CHART XIII.
Expressions of the Nose.

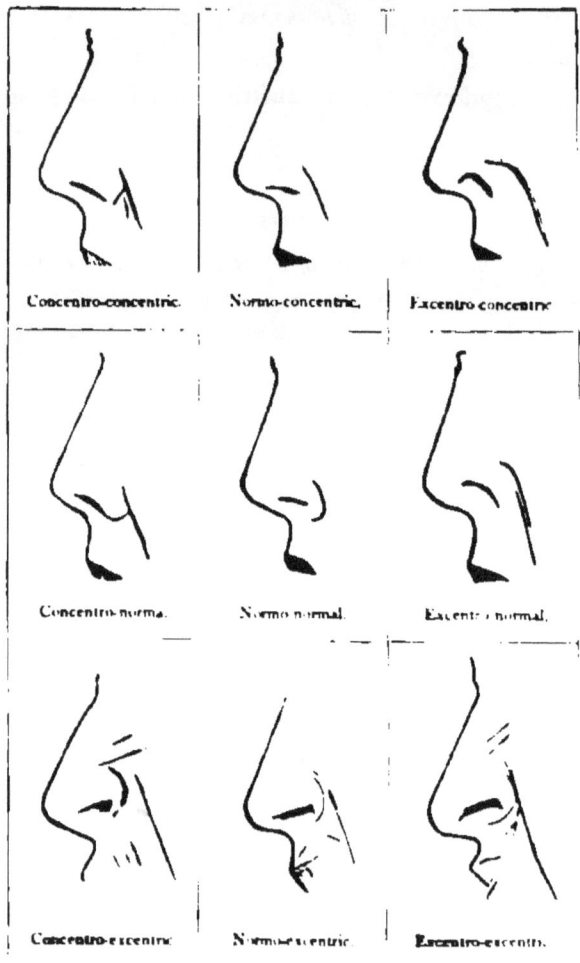

LESSON XVII.

THE LIPS AND THE JAW.

1. Lower jaw — energy in force;
2. Upper lip — sensitiveness in force;
3. Lower lip — will in force.

THE LOWER JAW.

The jaw slightly dropped — suspension of energy in force;

The jaw entirely dropped and back — paralysis of energy in force;

Jaw brought rigidly up and forward — exaltation of energy in force.

EXPRESSIONS OF THE MOUTH.

I.

Action: nor.-nor.
Signification: abandon, suspense.
Description of action: lips slightly parted.

II.

Action: con.-nor.
Signification: firmness.
Description of action: lips closely shut.

III.

Action: ex.-nor.

Signification: astonishment.

Description of action: lips completely apart.

IV.

Action: nor.-con.

Signification: disapproval plus abandon = grief.

Description of action: lips slightly apart, corners of mouth depressed.

V.

Action: con.-con.

Signification: disapproval plus firmness = discontent.

Description of action: lips closely shut, corners depressed.

VI.

Action: ex.-con.

Signification: disapproval plus astonishment = horror.

Description of action: lips completely apart, corners depressed.

VII.

Action: nor.-ex.

Signification: approval plus abandon = joy, pleasure.

THE LIPS AND THE JAW. 163

Description of action: lips slightly apart, corners of mouth raised.

VIII.

Action: con.-ex.

Signification: approval.

Description of action: lips closely shut, corners of mouth raised.

IX.

Action: ex.-ex.

Signification: approval plus astonishment = hilarity, laughter.

Description of action: lips completely apart, corners raised.

ÆSTHETIC GYMNASTICS.

Exercise.

Practice the various expressions contained in the chart of the mouth, passing in succession from one to the other. (See Chart XIV, page 164.)

CHART XIV.
Expressions of the Mouth.

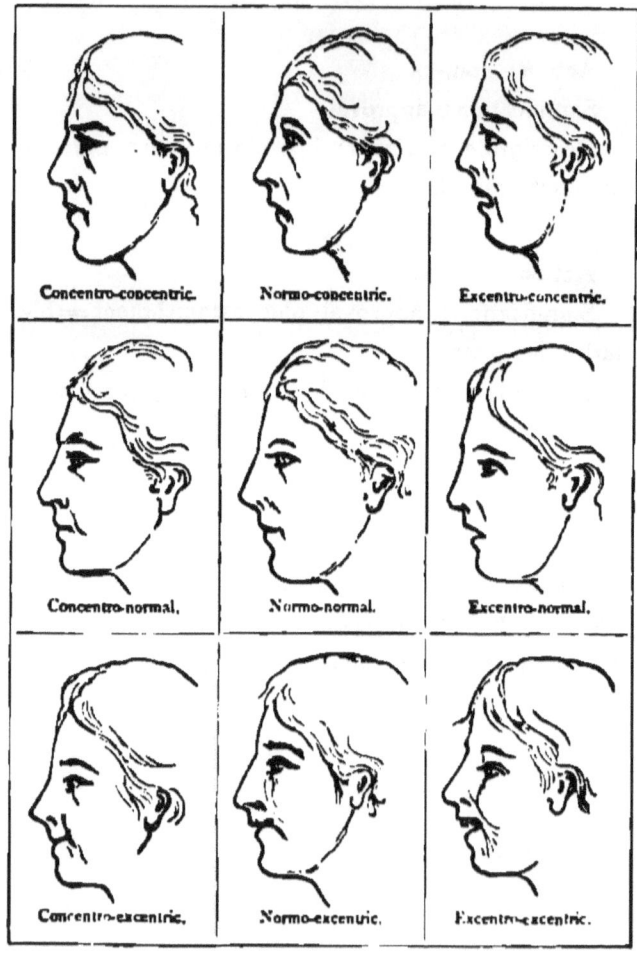

Grammar of Pantomime.

LESSON XVIII.

GRAMMAR OF PANTOMIME.

There are nine laws that govern the significance of motion in the human body, namely:

1. Altitude;
2. Force;
3. Motion;
4. Sequence;
5. Direction;
6. Form;
7. Velocity;
8. Reaction;
9. Extension.

The three primary laws are: (1) Altitude; (2) Force; (3) Motion.

LAW OF ALTITUDE.

Positive assertion rises;
Negative assertion falls.
The different degrees signify:

1. Probability;

2. Possibility;
3. Improbability;
4. Negation;
5. Impossibility;
6. Assertion [level with shoulder line];
7. Evidence;
8. Certainty;
9. Absolute truth;

The first five are negative and fall from level ot shoulder line; the last three are positive and rise from level of shoulder line.

LAW OF FORCE.

Conscious strength assumes weak attitudes;
Conscious weakness assumes strong attitudes.
This is true spiritually as well as physically.

LAW OF MOTION.

Its Relation to Emotion.

Excitement or passion tends to expand gesture;
Thought or reflection tends to contract gesture;
Love or affection tends to moderate gesture.
Thus,—

Passion tends to extreme expansion of the muscles;

Thought tends to extreme contraction of the muscles;

Affection tends to a happy medium of activity of the muscles.

The balance of passion and reason, in affection, constitutes the divinest emotion of being, and produces the most beautiful modulations of manner in the body.

An illustration of the tendency of passion to expand the body, is shown in the explosion of anger.

An illustration of the tendency of thought to contract the body, is shown in the attitude of the student.

An illustration of the tendency of affection to a happy medium, is shown in the attitudes characteristic of love.

The battle of reason with passion, in gesture, is one of the strongest forms of pantomime.

ILLUSTRATION.—Listening to a speech which excites passion, reason, trying to suppress the passion, contracts the form gradually. Those thermometers of passion, the nostrils and the upper lids, will indicate the passion. The mouth will contract, so will the hands and whole body. This will go on until the force of passion exceeds the force of reason in the will; then comes the explosion of passion, by the sudden and vehement expansion of the gesture.

DELSARTE SYSTEM.

LAW OF SEQUENCE.

"Let your attitude, gesture and face foretell what you would make felt."—*Delsarte.*

Expression of face precedes gesture, and gesture precedes speech.

This law illustrates the relation of pantomime to speech. It is a very important one. In considering the two languages of emotion, the verbal and the pantomimic, the latter is revelatory of the true man; while the verbal is more or less artificial. It takes many words to say what a single look reveals. Gesture is the lightning, speech the thunder; thus gesture should precede speech.

The gesture shows the emotional condition from which the words flow, and justifies them.

The eye is the centre of mental significance in expression. The centre of gravity is the vital centre. As the mind is first impressed and the passions are thence aroused, the eye should indicate attention or intention first; then the centre of gravity; then gesticulation; then articulation

LAW OF DIRECTION.

Lengths are passional;
Heights and depths are intellectual;
Breadths are volitional.

These facts apply both to the attitudes and inflections.

LAW OF FORM.

Straight form is vital;
Circular form is mental;
Spiral form is moral, mystic.

LAW OF VELOCITY.

"Gesture is melodic or inflective through the richness of its forms; harmonic through the multiplicity of parts that unite simultaneously to produce it. Gesture is rhythmic through its movement more or less slow, or more or less rapid. The law is thus formulated:

"The rhythm of gesture is proportional to the mass to be moved. This law is based upon the vibration of the pendulum. Great levers have slow movements; small agents more rapid ones." —*Delaumosne on Delsarte.*

"Rhythm is the form of movement.
"Melody is that which distinguishes.
"Harmony is that which conjoins." — *Delsarte.*

Velocity is in proportion to the mass moved and the force moving.

Agents of expression with short radii move faster than those with long radii.

In proportion to the depth and majesty of the *emotion*, is the deliberation and slowness of the *motion;* and, *vice versa*, in proportion to the superficiality and explosiveness of the *emotion*, will be the velocity of its expression in *motion*.

LAW OF REACTION.

"Every object of agreeable or disagreeable aspect which surprises us, makes the body recoil. The degree of reaction should be proportionate to the degree of emotion caused by the sight of the object."—*Delsarte.*

Every extreme of emotion tends to react to its opposite.

Concentrated passion tends to explosion; explosion to prostration. Thus the only emotion which does not tend to its own destruction, is that which is perfectly poised.

LAW OF EXTENSION.

The extension of a gesture is in proportion to the surrender of the will in emotion.

Finally, there remain but three additional great laws to consider, namely:

1. Opposition;
2. Evolution;
3. Trinity.

LAW OF OPPOSITION.

"When two limbs follow the same direction, they cannot be simultaneous without an injury to the law of opposition. Therefore, direct movements should be successive and opposite movements simultaneous."—*Delsarte.*

"Delsarte himself tells us that he studied the poses of the statues of antiquity for fifteen years. It was in consequence of this period of study that the master condemned the parallel movement of the limbs in gesture, and recommended attitudes which he called inverse."—*Arnaud on Delsarte.*

The law is thus stated:

*Simultaneous movement must be made in opposition;
Successive movement should be parallel.*

It is the law of harmony in music; symmetry in form; grace in movement; equilibrium; repose in action; sex; unity, as illustrated by the magnetic poles, or by the necessity of opposition of form in things that are to unite.

This law applied to gesture sublimates it.

LAW OF EVOLUTION.

"*Evolutio—evolvere.* Act of unfolding or unrolling; hence, in process of growth, development; as the evolution of flower from the bud. A series of things unrolled."—*Webster's Dictionary.*

" Progression of the articulations of the limbs.

" Here follow the vital expression of the arm, and the progression through which it should pass in moving from one articulation to another.

" There are three great articular centres: The shoulder, elbow and wrist. Passional expression passes from the shoulder, where it is in the emotional state, to the elbow, where it is presented in the affectional state; then to the wrist and the thumb, where it is presented in the susceptive and volitional state."—*Delsarte.*

EXAMPLE.—Lift your arm, vital force in upper arm, forearm and hand decomposed. Then unbend elbow, vital force flowing into forearm. Then expand hand, vital force flowing into fingers,—all this being a gradual unrolling or evolution of vital force through the various articulations.

The law of evolution necessarily includes its opposite, viz., *involution*, from the Latin root *involvo*, to wrap or fold in. Given an extended gesture of the arm, vital force retires, first, from the hand; second, from forearm; third, from upper arm and shoulder. It is the correct use of this law which forms one of the principal elements in the production of perfect gesture.

LAW OF TRINITY.

"The principle of the system lies in the statement that there is in the world a universal formula which may be applied to all sciences, to all things possible.

"This formula is the trinity.

"What is requisite for the formation of a trinity?

"Three expressions are requisite, each presupposing and implying the other two. Each of the three terms must imply the other two. There must also be an absolute co-necessity between them. Thus, the three principles of our being, life, mind and soul, form a trinity.

"Why?

"Because life and mind are one and the same soul; soul and mind are one and the same life; life and soul are one and the same mind."
—*Delsarte*.

[The trinity-principle has been extensively treated in Lesson III.]

A Gamut of Expression in Pantomime.

LESSON XIX.

A GAMUT OF EXPRESSION IN PANTOMIME.

IMAGINARY SCENE I.

You are standing idly in a room; a step on the stairs attracts your attention. The door opens to admit a person for whom you have an affection. You greet this person in delighted surprise.

Pantomime I.

Assume attitude of legs con.-ex.; right leg strong. Attention called to noise on the right, you lift right ear, eyes turning left in opposition. Door opens. Eyes turn right toward object entering. Head follows in rotary motion, levelling gaze on object. Face assumes an expression of delighted surprise. Titillation of eyelids. Head lowers slightly toward object in tenderness, con.-con.; shoulder rising in opposition. Movement creeps down upper arm and turns eye of elbow toward object, thus asserting tenderness. This movement has slightly bent forearm as it hangs from elbow decomposed. Now unbend forearm. Rotary movement of wrist turns hand into relative attitude con.-ex. Hand then expands in conditional attitude ex.-nor., affection. During action of arm, head has been rising in its proportionate arc; it finishes in attitude con.-ex., abandonment to affection.

IMAGINARY SCENE II.

Receiving no response from the object of your greeting, you increase the courtesy of your salutation, with repeated assurance of your affection.

Pantomime 2.

From final attitude of Pantomime 1, head becomes con.-nor.; shoulder rises a trifle in opposition, showing sensibility. Head continues motion toward hand, which rises in relative attitude ex.-con. The motion now passes into torso and forearm; that is, the torso bends obliquely toward object in courteous reverence, forearm at the same time bending up until backs of fingers touch chin. Retaining that position, elbow is lifted out and up to level of shoulder; hand falls decomposed (similar to a motion in serpentine movement) and the head rotates to left in opposition. Head and arm now resume previous position. Torso and forearm unbend. Head rises as hand falls into relative attitude con.-ex., and expands into conditional attitude ex.-nor. of tenderness.

N. B.—The movement of elbow UP and OUT has signified: "I emphasize the assurance of my affection for you!" The elbow turned out, meaning tenderness, force, etc.

IMAGINARY SCENE III.

Your greeting increases in ardor. Receiving no response, you express surprise and affectionate protest.

Pantomime 3.

From final attitude of Pantomime 2, arm makes an upward movement of appellation, head dropping a little in opposition. Hand now expands into conditional attitude nor.-ex., animation; little finger pointing to normal zone of the torso. Forearm bends until little finger is brought to left side of normal zone. Simultaneously, torso has bent forward in opposition. A moment's pause, then the shoulders lift; face expresses surprise; hand drops decomposed, position of arm retained. Now sink elbow, pressing upper arm against side, throwing decomposed hand into relative attitude con.-nor. Unbend elbow, which throws hand out and up into relative attitude ex.-ex.

The torso has risen in opposition to forearm, the head to the hand, and the attitude is now one of affectionate protest.

IMAGINARY SCENE IV.

The object still shows great doubt of your love; and, consequently, you intensify your expressions of devotion.

Pantomime 4.

Retaining the attitude of protest, you now call in the aid of your left arm in order to intensify your expressions. Raise left arm almost to level of shoulder, attitude similar to that of right arm. Rotary movement of wrists turns hands into relative attitude con.-ex. Raise hands, relative attitude ex.-con.; bend forearms. Sink elbows, pressing them to sides; this brings fingers to armpits, torso bending in opposition to forearm, head to hand. Now both elbows rise up and out sideways. Hands fall decomposed; shoulders rise as head sinks lower. Attitude of legs changes to nor.-con. = concentration. Left leg strong, while elbows sink to sides. Forearms unbend as torso rises. Hands expand as head resumes its position. Shoulders drop and head rises to attitude ex.-ex. in assertion.

IMAGINARY SCENE V.

No effect is produced on object. In great surprise you ask the reason: " Does he think you guilty of some wrong to him?" You attest your innocence with great vehemence.

Pantomime 5.

From final attitude of Pantomime 4, right arm sweeps up in appellation. Head sinks toward object in opposition. Scrutiny and bewilderment depicted on face. A pause. Then both forearms bend, bringing hands vehemently to mental zone of torso. Upper arms level and parallel with shoulders. Shoulders rise; head sinks lower in opposition. Head rotates to left, followed by arms expanding into attitude ex.-nor. as head returns to right. Shoulders sink as head rises.

IMAGINARY SCENE VI.

Continued disbelief in your truth and innocence enrages you. You make, however, one final effort for self-control, but show extreme anger in bearing and face.

Pantomime 6.

From final attitude of Pantomime 5, right hand sweeps to left moral zone of torso. Hand clenches in conditional attitude con.-con. = concentrated passion, wrists turning in. At the same time, left elbow sinks, bringing wrist to level of hip. Hand clenched, wrist turned in = vital energy in concentration. Right knee has stiffened, making attitude of legs ex.-con. = defiance. Head has sunk in opposition to attitude ex.-con. = hate. A half spring on to right leg, as if to advance on object, is checked, resulting in a quick stamp only; then you recoil into attitude of legs ex.-con. At the spring, the hands have unclenched convulsively and rotated slightly, only to reclench at the recoil. Head has risen and sunk in opposition. The face expresses menace. The brows are lowered, the nostrils dilated, jaws clenched, etc.

IMAGINARY SCENE VII.

Your passion has now passed beyond your control, and you order the object of it to leave your presence.

Pantomime 7.

From final attitude of Pantomime 6, forearm* unbends into attitude of arms ex.-ex. Wrist rotates hand into relative attitude ex.-nor. Now make the movement described in Lesson VIII—the command to leave the room, to "Go!" When the arm is executing the last half of the movement "Go!"— *i. e.*, when the wrist is level with armpit,—change bearing to attitude of legs nor.-ex., animated attention. Right leg strong.

IMAGINARY SCENE VIII.

While gazing in anger at object, as in final attitude of Pantomime 7, its aspect changes into something

---

* Head "*right* forearm."

which paralyzes you with terror, appalls you, and fills you with loathing.

Pantomime 8.

Hands decompose and are brought tremblingly in front of face, palms outward as if to banish object from sight. Then elbows unbend, violently throwing arms out into attitude of extreme repulsion, ex.-ex. Hands relative attitude ex.-ex. Bearing changes to attitude of legs con.-con. = prostration. Left leg strong, head violently averted from object in ex.-con. = horror, hate.

IMAGINARY SCENE IX.

You glance toward object. To your amazement, another transformation has taken place. A vision of beauty is before you. Great astonishment depicted on face. You are attracted toward vision. It recedes. You beseech it to remain with you, but it vanishes, leaving you prostrate.

Pantomime 9.

Eye turns to object. Head follows. Bearing becomes ex.-con., left leg strong. Arms expand. Wrists turn hands palms up. Then arms are slowly brought to attitude of attraction, con.-ex., while the bearing becomes nor.-ex. Right leg strong. As the vision recedes, the bearing becomes ex.-ex., right leg strong, you gradually fall on left knee, arms rising in appellation to object as you kneel. Object vanishes. You faint, arms decomposing as you fall.

The Voice.

LESSON XX.

THE VOICE.

IN TONE AND WORD (*logos*).

In all that follows, wherever I can, I shall let Delsarte speak for himself. Of this division I am but the editor, glad of any scintillation from the brilliant spirit-light of the master.

In a previous lesson we found:

1. The voice,—vital;
2. The gesture,—moral;
3. The word,—mental;

the three thus revealing life, mind and soul.

RESPIRATION.

In regard to tone, its great essential, respiration, must first be studied. You remember, no doubt, three zones in the torso:

1. Mental,—chest;
2. Moral,—heart;
3. Vital,—abdomen.

Natural respiration brings into prominence, during inspiration, the vital zone. In the language of Delsarte:—

"It is the vital breath; but while you can sing with the natural respiration, it is rapidly exhausted if not augmented by additional inhalation; for it results in dryness and breathlessness, which cause suffering alike to singer and listener. The artificial breath, on the contrary, preserves the ease and freshness of the voice. The chest should be a passive agent."

Delsarte taught diaphragmatic breathing, which throws, during inspiration, the moral zone into greatest prominence.

Clavicular breathing brings the chest or mental zone into action. It is an hysteric method, only to be used when the dramatic situation demands sobbing, gasping utterance. Be very careful in its use; it indicates a mind unbalanced. It soon causes dizziness if performed in a sobbing manner. All great excitement and loss of control is betrayed pantomimically by the quick rise and fall of the chest in clavicular respiration.

For a complete and practical guide to the development and correct use of the respiratory and vocal organs, the student is referred to Guttmann's "Gymnastics of the Voice."*

---

* $1.25. Edgar S. Werner, Publisher, 48 University Place, New York.

VOICE-PRODUCTION.

In studying voice-production we must consider three essentials:

1. The lungs;
2. The larynx;
3. The pharynx, nose and mouth-cavities.

The lungs convey the air to the larynx, the vibrating agent; thence to the mouth-cavities, the reverberating or resonating agent.

Delsarte named the " direct attack " of the glottis, *martellato*, and compared it to pearls united by an invisible thread. According to him, each note should be produced by an elastic escapement. He cautioned against the squeezing out of the tone after it was produced. He taught that all intensity of effect was produced by a profound inspiration, expulsion, and finally this elastic escapement or articulate click of the glottis. The glottic stroke should be produced by explosion. The foregoing refers to vowels.

Upon this point the master directs that,—

" The initial consonant should be prepared the same way as the attack on the tone. Such is the concentration of the archer preparing to launch an arrow, of the runner about to leap a ditch."

Dragging of the voice before the consonant is

to be avoided. Delsarte's directions are to swell and diminish on a single note, E flat (of the medium); the intermediary notes will be sympathetically strengthened. This special exercise will prevent the separation of the registers and gain the mixed or heart-voice.

When this note has acquired broad and powerful tones, the development is to be communicated to the neighboring notes.

Delsarte says:

"If you would move others, put your heart in the place of your larynx; let your voice become a mysterious hand to caress the hearer.

"There are two kinds of loud voices: the vocally loud, which is the vulgar voice; and the dynamically loud, which is the powerful voice. A voice, however powerful it may be, should be inferior to the power which animates it."

QUALITY OF TONE.

The vowel sounds, being the forms of the openings of pharynx and mouth, affect the quality of tone. The mother vowel *a*, the broad Italian sound (*ah*), is normal; with an acute accent it becomes *á* (as in *at*), excentric; with a grave accent it becomes *à* (as in *awe*), concentric.

From these three *a's* spring the other simple vowel sounds, viz.:

Excentric.	Normal.	Concentric.
á	a	à
é	o	e
è	au	eu
i	ou	u

N. B.—Look in a French dictionary for the correct pronunciation of the foregoing sounds.

Practice on E flat (medium) the normal vowels. They give the mixed quality of tone; then couple with them the consonants *l*, *m*, *p*. When further advanced, practice on the chromatic scale these combinations. The excentric vowels give the physical quality of tone. The concentric give the mental tone. Once having secured and recognized the moral love-tone, the mental and physical vowels can be amalgamated into normal quality. For dramatic effect the power to take each quality at will is necessary.

POINTS OF REVERBERATION.

There are three significant points of reverberation in the mouth:

1. The physical in the pharynx;
2. The moral or normal in the palatine arch;
3. The mental back of the upper teeth.

The normal vowel emission is naturally directed to the palatine arch; the excentric to the pharynx; the concentric or mental to the back of the teeth.

The common street-vender, as he calls his wares, is an example of the physical emission and reverberation. When we are under the influence of physical emotion, our voices harmonize in expression. "Hoarse with passion" is a common phrase. This voice is sometimes very effective in dramatic expression, but, if much used, hoarseness is sure to be the consequence.

The mental voice expresses a hard, cold, scientific statement of facts.

COLOR OF TONE.

The voice is further colored by gesture. I have previously called your attention to the fact that the conditional attitudes of the hand sympathetically color the voice; and again, the expression of the face preceding the tone will color it. To quote Delsarte: —"The ravished listener should be dazzled by a song unheard as yet, but which he guesses or thinks he guesses."

Loudness of tone is inconsistent with true feeling. The more one is moved, the lower the utterance. The voice is brilliant when there is little emotion.

THE VOICE.

In deep feeling the heart seems to be in the throat and the voice is stifled. "The whining, tearful tone is always weak."—(Delsarte.)

INFLECTION.

We now approach a subject of great importance,—inflection. Inflection in gesture has been defined as a movement indicating a passing emotion. Inflection in voice also, subtly indicates each passing thought.

Hear again the master:—

"Persuade yourself that there are blind men and deaf men in your audience whom you must *move*, *interest* and *persuade!* Your inflection must become pantomime to the blind, and your pantomime, inflection to the deaf."

Inflections are rising, falling, or the voice rests in monotone. Thus they are excentric, concentric and normal. Combinations of these three produce the inflection named by English authorities circumflex.

The shade, a poetic accent, is rather felt than expressed. It must be innate; it can be named, but not learned. You may have heard a play, a song, many times, and its effect on you has been cold and barren; but, some day, under the inspiration of a creative touch, the dead ashes of your enthusiasm are fired by a living spark. The *feu sacré* of genius has fallen from Olympus and illumined all around.

"Accent is the modulation of the soul."—(Delsarte.)

Arnaud writes:

"Delsarte had established typical phrases, where the mere shade gave an appropriate meaning to every variety of impression and sentiment which can possibly be expressed by any one set of words. One of these phrases was this: 'This is a pretty dog.'

"A very talented young girl succeeded in giving to these words a great number of different modulations, expressing endearment, coaxing, admiration, ironical praise, pity and affection. Delsarte, with his far-reaching comprehension, conceived of more than 600 ways of differentiating these examples.

"The second phrase was: 'I did not tell you that I would not.'

"This time the words lent themselves to revealing, as the case might be, indifference, reproach, encouragement, the hesitation of a troubled mind."

The shade is intimately connected with the ellipsis which formed a most important part of Delsarte's method.

"The conjunction and interjection are elliptical; thus in the sentence, 'Ah! .... how miserable I am!' 'Ah!' should imply a painful situation before the explanatory words begin."—(Delsarte.)

The silence which follows "Ah!" must, however, be filled by a significant gesture.

PARTICULAR INFLECTIONS.

Under the head of particular inflections come:

1. Exclamations; a startled cry on *ah, eh,* or *oh.*
2. Cries; prolonged exclamations on *ah,* caused by acute pain, joy, fear. In violent pain produced by a physical cause, the exclamation starts from a deep sound, then strikes a high sound, then a medium tone in a circumflex manner.
3. Groans; formed by two successive sounds, a high and then a low sound. A constant and monotonous repetition of these tones produces the effect.
4. Lamentation; expressed by a sombre, lugubrious, big voice, expressing grief that cannot be repressed.
5. The sob is produced by a clavicular, hysteric breathing, in a succession of little vocalized inspirations followed by a long vocalized expiration.

N. B.—Clavicular breathing, the rise and fall of the chest, is a sign of excitement.

6. The sigh is the product of a long and slow inspiration followed by a sudden, faint-toned expiration.

7. The laugh is the product of a deep inspiration followed by a succession of short, quick explosive vocal expirations. The vowel used should be Italian *a* or *o*, prefixed by *h*, for a normal laugh.

8. Singing is the modulated voice. "Things said quietly should sing themselves in the utterance." — (Delsarte.)

N. B.—"Preparation for tone consists in deep breathing, depression of larynx, canalization of tongue."—(Delsarte.)

The late Prof. Lewis B. Monroe was an ardent student of Delsarte. Their minds were akin, and he welcomed every thought of the latter with great joy, for in himself he felt the reverberation. So I make no apology for here introducing a collection of notes from him.

PRINCIPLES OF EMPHASIS AND INFLECTION.

1. "The emphatic word is the one that suggests the main idea.

2. "Falling inflection expresses the will or knowledge of the speaker.

3. "Rising inflection defers to the hearer, or to the will of the hearer.

4. "Rising inflection is prospective.

5. "Falling inflection is retrospective.

6. "Monotone is suspensive.

7. "The slide always falls on the accented syllable of the word.

8. "A modifying phrase reverts by its pitch to the clause or word modified.

9. "Fact of negation in a sentence does not, as a rule, change the emphasis.

10. "Doubt about emphasis, greater includes the less. See which word will convey the idea or suggest the answer, and which words can be thrown away.

11. "Reiteration in emphasis requires the falling inflection.

12. "If the falling inflection is given, the subordinate clause must be lower in pitch; if the rising, the subordinate clause must be higher in pitch.

13. "Of falling inflections, the higher takes precedence.

14. "A concession followed by an opposing assertion takes the rising inflection.

15. "Rising circumflex may indicate a doubt."

THE WORD (*logos*).

Man communicates with his fellow-man in three ways:

    1. The voice;
    2. The gesture;

3. The word;
the different expressions of life, mind and soul.

Words are the combinations of vowels and consonants.

I here quote the late Dr. Guilmette's arrangement of vowels and consonants; it is invaluable.

CHART XV.—VOWELS.

Permutation of the Five Organic Vowel Sounds.

N. B.—Let there be a prompt and firm molding of the sounds, with "direct attack" of glottis.

a (ah), o (oh), e (eh), u (oo), i (ee).

I.	II.	III.
i e u a o	i u e a o	i o e u a
i e u o a	i u e o a	i o u a e
i e o u a	i u o a e	i o a u e

IV.	V.	VI.
i a e u o	e i u a o	e u i a o
i a u e o	e i a u o	e u a i o
i a o u e	e i o a u	e u o i a

VII.	VIII.	IX.
u i e a o	u a i e o	a i e u o
u i a e o	u a o i e	a i u o e
u e i o a	u o e a i	a e u o i

X.	XI.	XII.
a u i e o	o a e u i	o i e u a
a u o i e	o a i u e	o e i a u
a u e o i	o a e i u	o u e a i

[The sounds of the English vowels, according to Bell, are: "1—eel; 2—ill; 3—ale; 4—ell, ere; 5—an; 6—ask; 7—ah; 8—her; 9—up, urn; 10—on, all; 11—ore; 12—old; 13—pull, pool. U after a vocal consonant is u as in duty, literature; u after r is oo as in rue, true."]

CHART XVI.—CONSONANTS.

Permutations of the Labials, Linguals and Laryngeals.

I.

LINGUALS.

t l k r	k t l r
t k l r	r t l k
t r l k	k r t l
l t k r	r k l t

II.

LABIALS *p* AND *ſ* WITH **LARYNGEALS** *b* AND *g*.

p ſ b g	ſ g p b
p b ſ g	g ſ b p
p g ſ b	g b p ſ
ſ p b g	b p ſ g

III.

LABIAL *p* WITH **LINGUALS** *t* AND *k* AND **LARYNGEAL** *b*.

p t k b	b p t k
p k t b	k p b t
k b p t	b t k p
k t p b	t p k b

CLASSIFICATION OF THE ORGANIC LABIAL, LINGUAL AND LARYNGEAL ARTICULATIONS.

I.

Labial proper p—p;
Semi-labial f—f.

II.
LINGUAL.

Apex of the tongue straight, t—t hard;
Apex of the tongue curved, l—l soft;
Dorsum of the tongue arched, r—r hard, vibratory;
Apex of the tongue curved, r—r soft, vibratory.

III.
LARYNGEAL.

b—b; g—g; d—d; v—v.

DIRECTIONS FOR PRACTICE.

1. The principal laryngeal sound represented by the character *b* should, for the purpose of enlarging the chamber of the larynx, be practiced *forcibly*, several times a day. It is wrongly named a consonant.

2. Prefix the articulation of each of the above consonants to the closed organic vowel *i (ee)*, taking care to keep passive those vocal organs whose immediate use is not required. Let the mind be very

vigilant over the active organ, and none other, *taking care to retain it* for a second or more in its position after the articulation shall have been given.

3. The same rule should be strictly observed in the molding of the organic vowel sounds, otherwise a slurring and drawling of the vocal element will be the result, and a miserably defined vowel will result for speaker or singer.

4. The organic vowel sounds *a* and *o (ah* and *oh)* should be practiced upon a steady intonation, with the mouth widely opened and held firm by the introduction of the points of the first three fingers, and there retained during the molding of these vowel sounds. Use the same process for the vowels *e* and *u (eh* and *oo)*, with the points of two fingers holding the jaws firmly apart. Finally use one finger for *i (ee)*.

5. Practice chart of organic vowels with active whisper; then practice laryngeal *b*, without vocalization, on different notes of the scale, viz.: 1, 2, 3, 4, 5, 6, 7, 8; 1, 3, 5, 8; 1, 4, 6, 8.

6. Finally, essay the following lines, with strict regard to the molding of vowels and consonants, on the chromatic scale, rising a half tone at each italicized word and continuing the next line on that tone.

> "There stood an unsold captive in the *mart*,
> A gray-haired and majestical old man,
> Chain'd to a *pillar*. It was almost night,
> And the last seller from his place had *gone*,
> And not a sound was heard but of a dog
> Crunching beneath the stall a refuse *bone*,
> Or the dull echo from the pavement rung
> As the faint captive changed his weary *feet*."

"The initial consonant should be articulated distinctly; the strength of the word lies in it."—(Delsarte.)

It would be better, perhaps, to say the initial consonant of the root. The force of the consonant is subordinated to the degree of the idea it is called on to determine. One of the secrets of expression is in the time you hold the initial consonant of the root before articulation. That silence is the father of the word and justifies it. This brings us to the consideration of

THE THEORY OF DEGREES.

I shall quote entire from an old pupil of the master, Arnaud:

"In the Course of Applied Æsthetics, the theory of degrees was largely developed. To understand this theory—one of the most striking points in Delsarte's method, and original with him—one should have some idea of the grammar which he composed for the use of his pupils. All that is the very essence of language, that from which no language, no idiom can escape — the constituent parts of speech — are examined and investigated from a philosophic and psychologic point of view. Just as the author examined the constituent modalities of our being in the light of æsthetics, he seized the affinities between the laws of speech, as far as regards the voice — *logos* — and the moral manifestations of art. I will only enter into these studies so far as they refer to the special field of æsthetics.

"In this category, we find the following definitions which serve to classify the quantitative values or degrees; that is, the extent assigned to each articulation or vocal emission to enable it to express the thoughts, sentiments and sensations of our being in their truth and proportionate intensity:

"1. *Substantive* is the name given to a group of appearances, to a totality of attributes.

"2. *Adjective* expresses ideas, simple, abstract, general and modificative; it is an abstraction in the substantive.

"3. *Verb* is the word that affirms the existence and the coëxistence between the being existing and its manner of existing.

"4. The *participle* alone is a sign of action.

"5, 6, 7. The *article*, *pronoun* and *preposition* fit into the common definitions.

"8. The *adverb* is the adjective of the adjective and of the participle (in so far as it is an attribute of the verb); it modifies them both, and is not modifiable by either of them; it is a sign of proportion, an intellectual compass.

"9. The *conjunction* has the same function as the preposition; it unites one object to another object, but it differs from it, inasmuch as the preposition has but a single word for its antecedent, and a single word for its objective case, while the conjunction has an entire phrase for antecedent, and the same for complement. It characterizes the point of view under the sway of which the relation should be regarded: restrictive, as *but*; hypothetical or conditional, as *if*; conclusive, as *then*, etc. The conjunction presents a general view to our thought; it is the reunion of scattered facts; it is essentially elliptical.

"10. The *interjection* responds to those circumstances where the soul, moved and shaken by a crowd of emotions at once, feels that by uttering a phrase it would be far from expressing what it experiences. It then exhales a sound, and confides to gesture the transmission of its emotion.

"The interjection is essentially elliptical, because,

expressing nothing in itself, it expresses at the time all that the gesture desires it to express, for ellipsis is a hidden sense, the revelation of which belongs exclusively to gesture.

"It must first be noted that these degrees are numbered from one to nine, and that, of all the grammatical values defined, the conjunction, interjection and adverb are classed highest.

"Delsarte made the following experiment one day in the 'Circle of Learned Societies' during a lecture:

"'Which word,' he asked his audience, 'requires most emphasis in the lines—

"'"The wave draws near, it breaks, and vomits up before our eyes,
Amid the surging foam, a monster huge of size."'

"The absence of any rule applicable to the subject caused the most complete anarchy among the listeners. One thought that the word to be emphasized must be *monster*—as indicating an object of terror; another gave the preference to the adjective *huge;* still another thought that *vomits* demanded the most expressive accent, from the ugliness of that which it expresses.

"Delsarte repeated the lines:

"'"The wave draws near, it breaks, and . . . . . vomits up before our eyes."'

"It was on the word *and* that he concentrated all the force of his accent; but giving it, by gesture, voice and facial expression, all the significance lacking to that particle, colorless in itself, as he pronounced the word, the fixity of his gaze, his trembling hands, his body shrinking back into itself, while his feet seemed riveted to the earth, all presaged something terrible and frightful. He saw what he was about to relate, he made you see it; his words had only to specify the fact, and to justify the emotion which had accumulated in the interval.

"But this particle, which here allows of eight degrees, is much diminished when it fills the office of a simple copulative. The extent of the word or syllable is always subordinate to the sense of the phrase; in the latter case it does not require more than the figure 2."

N. B. — Gesture and expression of face should always precede the pronunciation of the initial consonant. It should justify its value. The inflection of the voice should also harmonize with the value.

Delsarte continues:

"On retracing in my memory the walks I had taken in the Tuileries, I was struck by an important fact amidst the phenomena called up: the voice of the nurse or mother, when she caressed her child, invariably assumed the double character of tenuity and acuteness. It was in a voice equally sweet and high-pitched that she uttered such words as these:

'How lovely he is!'—'Smile a little bit for mamma!' Now this caressing intonation, impressed by nature upon the upper notes of all these voices, forms a strange contrast to the direction which all singing-teachers agree in formulating; a direction which consists in augmenting the intensity of the sound in direct ratio to its acuteness. Thus, to them the entire law of vocal shades would consist in augmenting progressively the sound of the ascending phrase or scale, and diminishing in the same proportion for a descending scale. Now nature, by a thousand irrefutable examples, directs us to do the contrary, that is, she prescribes a decrease of intensity (in music, *decrescendo*) proportionate to the ascensional force of the sounds. I was, therefore, fully convinced that caressing, tender and gentle sentiments find their normal expression in *high* notes."

Delsarte was not yet satisfied; he felt there must be some truth in such a universally received law. He proceeds:

"I will knock unceasingly at the door of facts. I will question every phenomenon.

"I then perceived that my first affirmations were no better founded than those of the masters, whose theories I had attacked. The truth of the matter is that ascending progressions may arise from opposite shades of meaning. 'Therefore,' said I to myself, 'it is equally inadmissible to exclude either affirmation.'

"The law is necessarily complex: let us bring together, that we may seize them as a whole, both the contrary expressions and the circumstances which produce them.

"Vulgar and uncultured people, as well as children, act in regard to an ascensional progression in an inverse sense to well-educated, or, at any rate, affectionate persons, such as mothers, fond nurses, etc.

"But why this difference? What are its motive causes?

"'Ha!' I cried, as if struck by lightning, 'I've found the law! As with the movements of the head, *sensuality* and *tenderness*, these shades of meaning may be traced back to two distinct sources: *sentiment* and *passion*. It is sentiment which I have seen revealed in mothers; it is passion which we find in uncultured persons.'"

N. B.—The word passion here seems to signify impulse, excitement, vehemence.

"Sentiment and passion, then, proceed in an inverse way. Passion strengthens the voice in proportion as it rises, and sentiment, on the contrary, softens it in due ratio to its intensity."

Here follows Delsarte's formulation of the law of vocal proportions:

"Given a rising form, such as the ascending scale, there will be intensitive progression when this form should express passion (whether impulse, excitement or vehemence).

"There will be, on the other hand, a diminution of intensity where this form is caused by sentiment.

"Moreover, the application of this law is subject to quantitative expressions or shades.

"These quantitative shades or expressions result from the greatness or littleness of the being or objects to which the sounds relate. Thus we would not use the same tones for the words: 'Oh, what a pretty little girl!'—'What a lovely little flower!'— And: 'See that nice, fat peasant woman!'—'What a comfortable great house!'

"Thus, a gamut should be considered as a double scale of proportion, according to the theory indicated above."

These formulæ are applicable to the spoken phrase as well as to music.

DEGREES FOR MUSIC.

Laure de La Madelène reports Delsarte as saying: "Light and shade are not, as has been asserted, subject to the arbitration of inspiration; they are ruled by laws (for in art there is no phenomenon not subject to absolute mathematical laws). These laws, which it is most important to know, form the basis of the system.

"The sound of an ascending phrase does not necessarily increase in intensity; far from it; the opinion which makes it progressive is, six times out of seven, incorrect. It is only correct where no *repeated* note or *dissonant* note is encountered in the ascent. Then the intensity of the sound may be centred upon the culminating note: in that case we will call it

First Degree.

"If we find a note repeated in the rising phrase, that note must be made more intense than the highest note; it will become the principal note (the note upon which chief stress is to be laid, if we may so express it). The sound must diminish in proportion to its distance from this centre of expression, for in a musical phrase (as in a logical or mimetic phrase) there cannot be two chief values: the repeated note, however low, should, therefore, have

Two Degrees.

"If the repeated note be also the highest note, it will acquire new intensity: it must be marked as having

Three Degrees.

"(For we only repeat those things which are requisite or necessary: for instance, in conversation, if the person with whom you are talking seems absent-minded, and your remarks do not seem to be very important, you lay no stress upon them; but if you think your statement requires a hearing, you repeat your words in a louder tone and articulating more distinctly, in order that you may be heard and understood; in the same way, if you receive no answer to this appeal, upon repeating it you necessarily make some change in the conditions in which the first appeal was made: this change can only be a renewed augmentation of sound and a more marked articulation.)

"We may possibly find a dissonant note in the ascending phrase, preceding a repeating and culminating sound. This note could, then, have but one significance; the accident would give it the form of an adjective, and it would have, in the musical phrase, the value that an adjective would have in a logical or spoken phrase. Its intensity would, therefore, be greater than that of the highest repeated note: it would, therefore, take

Four Degrees.

"If the dissonant note is also the highest note, that fact would give it new intensity: it would then have

Five Degrees,

without affecting the intermediary values (the progressive value of the notes) — values determined by the position which the notes occupy in the scale of sounds: for in a phrase following a normal course,— that is, a phrase containing neither repeated notes nor dissonances, *ré* would exceed *do* in intensity, and *mi* would have more power than *ré;* and so on. And if, instead of following the diatonic or chromatic order, there be a solution of continuity — if, for instance, at a bound, we pass from the first to the fifth note in the gamut, the value of the three notes suppressed will not be destroyed, but *implied*, and the fifth note should be given the same intensity which it would have had if the three preceding notes had been uttered.

"The dissonant note, appearing in a rising phrase, may be repeated: in consequence of this repetition it would receive a greater value, which would give it

Six Degrees."

Arnaud tells us that Delsarte taught:—

"The root of the word appoggiatura being *appuyer* (to sustain), the chief importance should be given in the phrase, to appoggiatura, by extent and expression; the more so that this note is generally placed on a dissonance; and, according to this master's system, it is on the dissonance — and not at random and very frequently, as is the habit of many singers — that the powerful effect of the vibration of sound should be produced."

Finally, let me quote Delsarte's words in regard to musical signs:

"Signs are useful when the pupil begins his studies. To acquire freedom in the use of the mechanism, the pupil, before creating an artistic personality for himself, needs leading strings. He will never be really free until he can obey the will of a stranger; and when he has no teacher beside him, to whom he can refer and submit, indicative signs may, to a certain extent, supply the absent adviser; but, from the day that the student possesses freedom in the use of the instruments by means of which are revealed life, mind and soul, being an *artist*, he should no longer be compelled to hold to a strict observance of written signs. Otherwise he would be in danger of becoming a mere automaton, playing when the springs are pressed."

There, dear pupil, the master himself has advised the method of your use of all in the foregoing pages, not one word of which will be comprehended " save by a deed," as another great art-teacher, Ruskin, has said of the Book of books.

I cannot too strongly recommend the following method of utilizing the Delsarte System of Dramatic Expression, in the creation of character. While the wings of inspiration should never be clipped, still remember that the first essential of the power to command is the ability to obey; and the pupil in art cannot better test his power of conception than by forming it according to the high standard of perfect law. Remember, all great musicians have to stop the flight of Pegasus, while annoting their music in accordance with the laws of harmony and orchestration. The precision and thoroughness of music proves it a nobler art than the drama. It need not be so. You have it now in your power to uplift your own art-language. Will you do so? If you have the patience, obey the following directions:

Write one line of the text to be studied after the word "text"; above it write (1) v. c.=vocal color; (2) in.=inflection; (3) em.=emphasis; (4) being "text"; under "text" write (5) el.=ellipsis; (6) ex.=expression of face; (7) g.=gesture; (8) at.=attitude; (9) s. b.=stage business.

Below I give you an example:

SCENE FROM MACBETH.—Lady Macbeth speaks.

1. V. C. Some breath on moral tone;
2. In. Falling on "fail";
3. Em. On "fail";
4. Text. We *fail;*
5. El. We must resign ourselves to destiny;
6. Ex. Head bows, eyelids droop,—resignation;
7. G. Arms drop in abandon;
8. At. Concentro-excentric;
9. S. B Stands left of Macbeth.

N. B.—The ellipsis of a text *is* expressed by the gesture; so the signification of the two correspond. The expression of the face and the hand colors the tone; thus they, too, will correspond.

Color.

LESSON XXI.

COLOR.

So we are together again. The Christmas holidays have brought you. Lay aside your fur, for see how the snowflakes powder. Draw the armchair close to this great open fireplace; put your feet on the brass fender, and sit with me and watch the burning of the great log. What care we now for the cold outside? Listen to the sleigh-bells. You brought me this wreath? How it smells of the woods!

We are going to talk on color to-day—a fascinating subject. Do you recall how, some time ago, we touched on it in our illustrations of trinity? We found that the prismatic rays of the sun were clearly divided into three primary colors,—red, yellow and blue, the calorific, the colorific and the chemical ray. Colors derive their tints and hues from the refractions and reflections of the rays of heat and light from the sun, in varying intensity, combined more or less with darkness or blackness and shade. "There are two fundamental elements of color,—red, which is derived from the flaming light proceeding

NOTE.—According to notes of François Delsarte and the charts colored by Magdeleine Delsarte, yellow is moral or normal, the color of the soul; blue is mental or concentric, the color of the mind; red is vital or excentric, the color of the life. Modern chemical experiments and ancient symbolism seem to support the author's original statements.

from the heat, and white from light. All colors are modifications of these with obscurity or blackness." The trinity of red, yellow and blue constitute, combined, the unity of white or ordinary light. The red is the calorific or heating principle; the yellow is the colorific or light-giving principle; the blue is the chemical ray, in which the power of actinism or chemical action is found.

Red is significant of love; yellow of intelligence; blue of action or use. Red is thus moral; yellow is mental; blue is vital; or, red is normal, yellow is concentric, blue is excentric. "Celestial rosy red, love's proper hue," says Milton, in Paradise Lost.

N. B.—For the hues produced by their intermingling, look at the symbolic chart of color, page 226.

Colors had the same significance amongst all the ancient peoples. In Persia, the two principles of good and evil were symbolized under the two contrasts, light and darkness, white and black, from which all other color was derived. The color-language passed from India, China, Egypt and Greece, to Rome. It was revived in the Middle Ages, in the passionate, vital painting of the windows of the Gothic cathedrals and the walls of the churches of Venice,—"hues that have words and speak to us of heaven." Iris, the messenger of the gods and good tidings, has the rainbow for her girdle, the symbol of regeneration —the covenant between God and man. The robe of the Egyptian Isis sparkles and shines with all of nature's hues. "Osiris, the all-powerful god, gives light to Isis, who modifies it and transmits it by reflection to men. Isis is the earth, and her symbolic robe was the hieroglyphic of the material and of the spiritual worlds."

Heraldry is the last remnant of ancient symbolism. Every genuine old coat of arms was an utterance of chivalric honor to its wearer.

We all know there is symbolic meaning attached to the colors of a knight's shield, though the origin of such meaning seems to be lost in antiquity. Aztec paintings indicated these significations. Let me read you this from Ruskin:

"Whether derived from the quarterings of the knight's shield, or from what other source I know not; but there is one magnificent attribute of the coloring of the late twelfth, the whole thirteenth and the early fourteenth century, which I do not find definitely in any previous work nor afterward in general art, though constantly and necessarily in that of great colorists, namely, the union of one color with another by reciprocal interference; that is to say, if a mass of red is to be set beside a mass of blue, a piece of the red will be carried into the blue, and a piece of the blue carried into the red; sometimes in nearly equal portions, as in a shield divided into four quarters, of which the uppermost on one side will be of the same color as the lowermost on the other; sometimes in smaller fragments; but, in the periods above named, always definitely and grandly, though in a thousand various ways. And I call it a magnificent principle, for it is an eternal and a universal one, not in art only, but in human life. It is the great principle of *brotherhood*, not by equality, nor by likeness, but by giving and receiving;—the souls that are unlike, and the nations that are unlike, and the natures that are unlike, being bound into one noble whole by each receiving something from and of the other's gifts and the other's glory. . . . I have long believed that in whatever has been made by the Deity externally delightful to the human sense of beauty, there is some type of God's nature or of God's laws; nor are any of His laws, in one sense, greater than the appointment that the most lovely and perfect unity shall be obtained by the taking of one nature into another. I trespass upon too high ground; and yet I cannot fully show the reader the extent of this law, but by leading him thus far. And it is just because it is so vast and so awful a law, that it has rule over the smallest things; and there is not a vein of color on the lightest leaf which the spring winds are at this moment unfolding in the fields around us, but it is an illustration of an ordainment to which the earth and its creatures owe their continuance and their redemption."

Ah! you draw a long breath; so do I. To me Ruskin has ever been an apostle of light and beauty and truth. "Wherever literature assuages woe" his burning words will fire and cheer.

The selam or nosegay of the Arabs is emblematic. The Koran mystically says: "The colors which the earth displays to our eyes are manifest signs for those who think."

"The colors which appear on the earth correspond to the colors which the seer beholds in the world of spirits, where everything is spiritual and, consequently, significative. Such is, at least, the origin of the symbolical meaning of colors in the books of the prophets and the Apocalypse." (Portal's *Des Couleurs Symboliques*.)

Red in the original tongue is called *adam*, signifying good.

Madeley, in his "Science of Correspondences," says:

"The twelve stones in the urim and thummim are

representative of all the varieties of divine truth; brilliant, transparent, sparkling, glowing with inward radiant principles of love, charity, goodness and benevolence, of which they are but the outward forms. They were ordered by express divine command to be arranged in trines and worn on the breast or over the heart of the high priest when he entered the tabernacle. They were divided into four orders of trines, distinctly significative of the twofold constitution of the internal and external man; each trine having especial relation to the three degrees of the mind and life, and the signification of each stone being determined by its color and by its place. This may be seen more clearly from the following arrangement:

1st row: Sardius, topaz, carbuncle.
Reuben; Simeon; Levi;

signifying and representing the three degrees of celestial goodness in the internal will, with their purity and burning brilliancy. (Topaz was evidently red.)

2nd row: Emerald, sapphire, diamond.
Judah; Dan; Naphtali;

signifying and representing the three degrees of celestial wisdom in the internal understanding, with their transparent and sparkling lustre.

3rd row: Ligure,   agate,   amethyst.
        Gad;   Asher;   Issachar;
signifying and representing the three degrees of spiritual love or charity which are active in the external will, but modified in brilliancy.

4th row: Beryl,   onyx,   jasper.
        Zebulon; Joseph;   Benjamin;
signifying and representing the three degrees of faith or knowledge in the external understanding, less transparent and more opaque than the three degrees of internal wisdom.

"Similar things are signified in the order of the stones in the foundations of the new Jerusalem."

"Colors have an influence on the passions; and they, as well as their harmonies, have relation to moral and spiritual affections."—(St. Pierre's "Studies of Nature.")

There, have I not given you quite a universal budget? When next we meet, bring a nosegay, arranged in colors that speak. Ah! while chatting our flaming log has changed to radiant coals. Observe the burning red thrilled and penetrated with yellow luminous light. Its vivid existence is shown in the tiny bluish flame which, like an aura, emanates from its consuming life.

CHART XVII.
Symbolic Colors.

mento-mental yellow plus yellow = yellow. concentro-concentric.	moro-mental red in yellow = orange. normo-concentric.	vito-mental blue in yellow = green (light). excentro-concentric.
mento-moral yellow In red = scarlet. concentro-normal.	moro-moral red plus red = red. normo-normal.	vito-moral blue in red = purple. excentro-normal.
mento-vital yellow in blue = green (dark). concentro-excentric.	moro-vital red in blue = violet. normo-excentric.	vito-vital blue plus blue = indigo. excentro-excentric.

Red = Love;
Yellow = Intelligence;
Blue = Power.

Parting Advice.

Before we part, let me tell you how to use our previous lessons.

First, they place you in possession of the highest standards by which to judge all great works. Next, they start you on your art-pilgrimage; but they will not take you all the way. The greatest art-work is only produced under the inspiration of such supreme laws, that man cannot voluntarily command it.

Practice all of the æsthetic gymnastics, use all the charts, but as gymnastics only. Never, in creating a role, make them your masters by a voluntary seeking of their attitudes in symbolic meaning. As a standard of criticism of sculpture, painting and acting, they have great use; yet here let me recall an anecdote:

"Haydn had agreed to give some lessons in counterpoint to an English nobleman. 'For our first lesson,' said the pupil, already learned in the art, drawing at the same time a quatuor of Haydn's from his pocket, 'for our first lesson may we examine this quatuor; and will you tell me the reasons of certain modulations which I cannot entirely approve because they are contrary to the principles?' Haydn, a little surprised, declared himself ready to answer. The nobleman began, and at the very first measures found matter for objection. Haydn found himself much embarrassed, and answered always, 'I have done that because it has a good effect. I put that passage there because it does well.' The Englishman, who judged that these answers proved nothing, recommenced his proofs and demonstrated to him, by very good reasons, that his quatuor was good for nothing. 'But, my lord, arrange this quatuor, then, to your fancy; play it so and you will see which of the two ways is the best.' 'But why is yours the best which is contrary to the rules?' "'Because it is the pleasantest.' Haydn at last lost patience and said: 'I see, my lord, it is you who have the goodness to give lessons to me, and, truly, I am forced to confess to you that I do not deserve the honor.' The partisan of the rules departed, still astonished that in following the rules to the letter one cannot infallibly produce a Matrimonio Segreto." (De Stendhal's *Vies de Haydn, de Mozart et de Metastase.*)

Ruskin adds to this:

"This anecdote, whether in all parts true or not, is in its tendency most instructive, except only in that it makes one false inference or admission; namely, that a good composition can be contrary to the rules. It may be contrary to certain principles supposed, in ignorance, to be general, but every great composition is in harmony with all true rules and involves thousands too delicate for ear, or eye, or thought to trace; still, it is possible to reason with infinite pleasure and profit about these principles, when the thing is once done; only all our reasoning will not enable any one to do another thing like it, because all reasoning falls short of the divine instinct. Thus we may reason wisely over the way a bee builds his comb, and be profited by finding out certain things about the angles of it; but the bee knows nothing about those matters. It builds its court in a far more inevitable way. And, from a bee to Paul Veronese, all master-workers work with this awful, this inspired unconsciousness."

You will not think me egotistical if I relate my own experience. When a student, I was an enthusiast on this subject of method. I worked at it, I thought of it, I dreamed it night and day; but I have never consciously used it in public work. And my best results have been attained when I, a passive subject, obeyed an inner inspiration coming from whence I know not and urging me on to results I had not aimed at. This, in my own modest efforts, has been my experience: how much more must it be the experience of great artists! Then why study?

Because the fruit, the flower, the child needs cultivation for development. Favorable circumstances, resolution and industry can do much; they determine as to whether the poor fruit shall fall and die, or expand into velvet softness; whether the flower shall wither ere it blossom; whether the child shall reflect heaven's light or earth's blackness. And now, let me conclude this by quotations from Ruskin just as applicable to oratory and acting as to the sister arts, writing and painting.

"Only according to his own nobleness is an artist's power of entering into the hearts of noble persons, and the general character of his dream of them.

"He who habituates himself in his daily life to seek for the stern facts in whatever he hears or sees, will have these facts again brought before him by the involuntary imaginative power in their noblest associations. And he who seeks for frivolities and fallacies will have frivolities and fallacies again presented to him in his dreams. Now, therefore, observe the main conclusions which follow from these two conditions attached always to art of this kind.

"First, it is to be taken straight from nature." (Delsarte studied for fifty years from nature, and so guides the beginner to truth. He rejected the traditional methods of movement taught in the Conservatoire.) "It is to be the plain narration of something the painter or writer saw. All great men see what they paint before they paint it, see it in a perfectly passive manner,—cannot help seeing it if they would; whether in their mind's eye or in bodily fact does not matter; very often the mental vision is, I believe, in men of imagination, clearer than the bodily one; but vision it is of one kind or another, —the whole scene, character, or incident passing before them as in second sight, whether they will or no, and requiring them to paint it as they see it; they not daring under the might of its presence to alter one jot or tittle of it as they write it down or paint it down. Therefore it is, that every system of teaching is false which holds forth 'great art' as in any wise to be taught to students or even to be aimed at by them. Great art is precisely that which never was, nor will be taught. It is preëminently and finally the expression of the spirits of great men; and without holding out to him as a possible or even probable result that he shall ever paint like Titian or carve like Michael Angelo, enforces upon him the manifest possibility and assured duty of endeavoring to draw in a manner at least honest and intelligible and cultivates in him those general characteristics of heart, sincerities of thought, and graces of habit which are likely to lead him throughout life to prefer openness to affectation, realities to shadows and beauty to corruption."

We have finished our task,—nay pleasure. Goodbye, little book; we are sorry to part. While with you, the living, loving spirit of the master, inspirer of my girlish dreams, dear companion always, has seemed beside me. Deep down, impressed on heart and mind, two names I find emblazoned,—

Delsarte—Ruskin.

Kindred spirits, masters mine, your thoughts, like grand old music, reverberate through my being. To one and all I bow and say, Amen. Your keen white souls, God's madmen are ye, have ever cried, —" On, youthful pilgrim!" Beauty's torch must be fired in a flaming heart. True art is but the soul's

"BEHOLD IT IS I."

Order of Exercises.

ORDER OF EXERCISES FOR SYSTEMATIC PRACTICE.

DECOMPOSING EXERCISES.

1. Fingers — one exercise.
2. Hand — one exercise.
3. Forearm — one exercise.
4. Entire arm — three exercises.
5. Head — two exercises; (*a*) dropped forward, (*b*) dropped back.
6. Torso — one exercise.
7. Foot — one exercise.
8. Lower leg — one exercise.
9. Entire leg — one exercise.
10. Entire body — one exercise.
11. Eyelids — one exercise.
12. Lower jaw — one exercise.

BEARING.

1. Harmonic bearing in standing attitude nor.-nor.
2. Harmonic bearing in attitude nor.-con.
3. Harmonic bearing in attitude nor.-ex.

4. Harmonic bearing in attitude con.-con.

5. Harmonic bearing in attitude ex.-ex.

6. Harmonic bearing in attitude con.-ex.

7. Harmonic bearing in attitude ex.-con.

8. Harmonic bearing when seated; (*a*) forward; (*b*) back; (*c*) sideways; (*d*) obliquely forward and back.

WALKING.

1. Take a long tape, mark the length of two of your feet on it. Pin it in front of a long mirror. Walk on it, letting the heel fall on the mark each step.

2. Observe harmonic bearing while in motion.

3. Lift the thigh, unbend the knee, plant the foot, let the torso lead.

4. Walk with a book on your head.

ARM-MOVEMENTS.

1. Sink wrist.

2. Wave arm through the air, letting the hand hang a dead weight. The hand will float as a feather. Keep the elbow stiff.

3. Evolution of vital force in arm-movement;

(*a*) lift upper arm; (*b*) unbend elbow; (*c*) expand hand.

4. Evolution of force in every altitude in lengths.
5. Evolution of force in every altitude in breadths.

N. B.—Lengths and breadths until heights and depths are reached.

6. Expand hand from closed fist, gradually opening the fingers, taking care that the thumb shall oppose the two middle fingers.
7. Serpentine movement.
8. Spiral movement.
9. Commanding movement.

N. B.—The serpentine movement is in the breadths; the spiral movement is in the heights; the commanding movement is in the lengths.

10. Raise the arm in evolution of motion; expand the hand into Definition; bring down in Teacher's Affirmation.
11. Raise the arm; expand the hand into Protection; bring down in Patron's Affirmation.
12. Raise the arm; expand the hand in Support; bring down in Champion's Affirmation.
13. Raise the arm; expand the hand in Limitation; bring down in Conservative's Affirmation.

14. Raise the arm; expand the hand in Despot's attitude; bring down in Tyrant's Affirmation.

15. Raise the arm; expand the hand in Mystic attitude; bring down in Seer's Affirmation.

16. Raise the arm; expand the hand in Exposition; bring down in Saint's Affirmation.

17. Raise the arm; expand the hand in Protest attitude; bring down in Orator's Affirmation.

18. Raise the arm; expand the hand in Bigot's attitude; bring down in Bigot's Affirmation.

19. Practice the nine affirmations with bent arm, as hand-movements.

20. Raise the arm, hand dead; rotate arm.

21. Raise the arm; sink wrist; rotate arm.

22. Practice the sinking of the wrist, and rotation with elbows bent and near sides.

23. Rise upon toes.

24. Poise forward and back from heels to balls of feet and back to heels.

25. Poise from ex.-con. attitude to nor.-ex.

26. Stand in attitude nor.-nor.; then poise from left to right and *vice versa*, slowly changing the centre of gravity.

27. Pivot (*a*) to right; (*b*) to left; (*c*) half-way round.

28. Gladiator oppositions.

29. Primary oppositions of head and arm.

30. Waist rotation in opposition to head rotation.

N. B.—The head rotates to the side of the strong leg.

31. Arm-gestures from significant zones.

32. Involution of body.

33. Evolution of body.

34. Bowing in opposition; as the knee sinks back, the torso bends forward and the head rises.

35. Bowing in successive movement; the eyes droop, then the head bows and the torso inclines.

36. Kneeling.

37. Falling.

38. Rotation of head in the various attitudes without changing the significant angle.

39. Gamut of expression in motion.

BREATHING EXERCISES.

1. Simple vital breathing; bring into prominence vital or excentric zone.

2. Artistic breathing; bring into prominence moral or normal zone.

3. Mental breathing; bring into prominence mental or concentric zone.

4. Normal breathing; then count one to ten, taking a short breath between each number, pronouncing the number with "direct attack" of glottis.

5. Normal breathing; hold breath, move arms vigorously in all directions.

6. Normal breathing; hold breath until you feel a warm current within, then exhale very slowly.

7. Inhale slowly through the nostrils, as if gently sniffing a nosegay, then exhale as slowly.

N. B.—Always inhale through the nostrils when possible in speaking and singing.

8. Inhale very slowly through the lips held as if whistling, walking quickly and moving arms vigorously; exhale slowly, continuing the arm and leg movement.

VOWEL AND CONSONANT ARTICULATION.

1. "Direct attack" of the glottis on charts of organic vowels.

2. Preparation for consonant articulation.

3. Combinations of vowels and consonants.

4. Chromatic scale on organic vowels.

5. Chromatic scale on *Sta-bat-ma-ter-do-lo-ro-sa-Jux-ta-cru-cem-la-cri-mo-sa-dum-pen-de-bat-fi-li-us*. Pronounce with the organic vowel molding.

6. Practice verse from "Parrhasius;" (*a*) in whisper; (*b*) in aspirate; (*c*) with normal tone, rising a note on each marked word.

7. Practice "Do you think so?" coloring the tone with the conditional attitudes of the hand.

8. Crescendo and diminuendo on *E* flat (medium) in the moral or heart-tone.

9. (*a*) Descend from *E* flat (medium) on the scale in the heart-tone; (*b*) ascend from *E* flat (medium) on the scale in the normal or heart-tone.

10. Practice coloring the tone with the various pantomimic expressions of the body, taking any word or phrase, as "Stop!" "Hold!" "I will not do it!" etc.

BELL'S VOWEL TABLE.

1—eel;
2—ill;
3—ale;
4—ell, ere;
5—an;
6—ask;
7—ah;
8—her;
9—up, urn;
10—on, all;
11—ore;
12—old;
13—pull, pool.

U after a vocal consonant is *u* as in duty, literature; *u* after *r* is *oo* as in rue, true.

BELL'S CONSONANT TABLE.

	Breath.	Voice.	Nasal Voice.
Lips {	p	b	m
	wh	w	
	f	v	
Point of tongue {	t	d	n
	s	z	
	th(in)	th(en)	
	r (rough)	r (smooth)	
	l		
Top of tongue {	sh	zh	
	y		
Back of tongue.	k	g	ng

J or soft g = dzh; ch = tsh (as in church); qu = kw; ph = f.

VERSES FROM PARRHASIUS.

There stood an unsold captive in the *mart*,
A grey-haired and majestical old man,
Chain'd to a *pillar*.   It was almost night,
And the last seller from his place had *gone*,
And not a sound was heard but of a dog
Crunching beneath the stall a refuse *bone*,
Or the dull echo from the pavement rung,
As the faint captive changed his weary *feet*.
'Twas evening, and the half descended sun
Tipp'd with a golden fire the many domes
Of *Athens*, and a yellow atmosphere
Lay rich and dusky in the shaded street
Through which the captive *gazed*.
The golden light into the painter's room
Stream'd *richly*, and the hidden colors stole
From the dark pictures radiantly *forth*,
And in the soft and dewy atmosphere
Like forms and landscapes magical they *lay*.

Index.

Index.

INDEX.

A.

	PAGE.
Abbreviations, explanation of	66
Accent	194
Action colored by habit	65
Adjective	204
Adverb	205
Advice to those appearing in public	79
Æsthetics, definition of	57
Æsthetic gymnastics, aim of	40
how to practice	227
talk	11, 17, 20, 27, 31, 40, 57, 71, 73
exercises for practice	12, 18, 49, 66, 73, 83, 95, 101, 108, 113
	117, 124, 134, 140, 151, 158, 163, 177
Affection, tendency of	169
Agate	225
Age, tendency of the	78
Agnostic attitude	68
Alger, W. R.	8
Amethyst	225
Anatomy, definition of	59
Ankle	49
Apocalypse, symbolic meaning of colors in	223
Apollo	32
Belvedere	20
Appoggiatura	213
Arm, sections of	41, 45
articular centres of	42, 47, 107
attitudes of	111
inflections of	115
chart of movements of right	125
vital expression of	173

INDEX.

	PAGE.
Arnaud, Mme. Angelique, quotations from..17, 36, 37, 38, 172,	194
203,	214
Art, definition of............17,	58
reason for studying rules of............	79
object of............	59
great............	231
Article............	205
Articulation the language of reason............	36
situation of the great............	24
its sequential order............	170
classification of the different............	201
Artificial breath............	188
Artist, an, and society............	28
necessity for nobleness of character in an............	230
Attitude, law of............	167
dignity of............	19
inverse............	172
Aztec painting............	221

B.

Beauty, line of............	18
is power............	21
Bell, A. Melville............	199
Beryl............	225
Best results, how attained............	229
Blue ray, necessary for fruit............	31
Body, opposition of parts of............	20
grand divisions of............	41
perfection and power of............	77
recoil of............	172
Breath, vital............	188
Brotherhood, principle of............	222
Brow, chart of............	143
Buckle............	5
Byron's tribute to a dog............	76

C.

Carbuncle............	224
Celestial wisdom, three degrees of............	224

INDEX.

	PAGE
Centres, great articular	173
Cerebration, unconscious, necessary	17
Charts...39, 72, 97, 125, 131, 135, 136, 142, 143, 152, 153, 154,	155
159, 164, 199, 200,	226
Delsarte's now given to the public for the first time	38
how to use	227
Cheek	129
Chin	129
Chest, in breathing	188
Circle-chart	125
Circumflex	193, 197
Clavicular breathing	188, 195
Color	219
language	220
Coloring, attribute of, in 12th, 13th and 14th centuries	221
Colors, their attributes	31
significations of	220
meaning among the ancients	220
chart of	226
Command "Go," the	104
Comte	5
Concentric motion, definition of	37
Conjunction	194, 205
Consonants, initial	180, 203
initial preceded by gesture	207
chart of	200
directions for practice of	201
Coriolanus, exiled	62
Correspondence, definition of	61
Criterion chart	39
terms, a shorthand of	40
Cry	195

D.

Decomposing exercises	11
Degrees, theory of	203
Deific essence	34
Delaumosne, l'Abbé	3
quotation from	171

260   INDEX.

	PAGE.
Delsarte, François, biographical sketch of	4
his efforts in behalf of dramatic art	5
his plans to come to America	7
quotations from ...24, 35, 47, 57, 60, 93, 94, 107, 108, 118,	170
171, 172, 173, 174, 188, 189, 190, 192, 193, 194, 196,	203
206, 207, 208, 210,	214
his fifty years of study	230
Delsarte system, not mechanical....60,	64
principle of 35,	174
one of the most striking points in	203
Demosthenes	79
De Stendhal, quotation from	228
Diamond	224
Diaphragmatic breathing	188
Direction, law of	170
Divine attributes, the	32
Divisions of the book:	
Introduction	1
Decomposing exercises	9
Harmonic poise of bearing	15
Basis of the system	29
Vital division	55
Moral division	119
Mental division	127
Grammar of pantomime	165
A gamut of expression in pantomime	175
The voice	185
Color	217
Order of exercises for practice	233
Dog's walk contrasted with man's	76
Dramatic art, the first step necessary for	11
necessity of practicing the technique of	215
Drunkenness, the gaze of	140
Dual principle	32
Dynamic wealth	24

E.

Ecstasy, the gaze of	140
Educational tendencies, harmful	40

	PAGE.
Egyptians, philosophy of the ancient	33
Elbow	108, 173
soul of the arm	46
as a thermometer	42, 48
signification of movement of	178
Ellipsis	194, 216
Emerald	224
Emotion, the only non-self-destructive	172
Emphasis, principles of	196, 197
doubt about	197
reiteration in	197
illustration in	206
Evolution, law of	173
Excentric motion, definition of	37
Exclamation	195
Expression, freeing the channels of	11
precedes gesture	170
movements of agents of	171
passional	173
a gamut of	177
one of the secrets of	203
Extension, law of	172
Eyeball, as an indicator	137
signification and action of	138
chart of	142
Eyebrow	143
signification and action of	144
charts of combinations of upper lid and	152, 153
chart of	154
Eyelid, upper	143, 146
lower	143, 148
simple combinations of brow and upper	148
Eyes	137
man has more white in	138
active agents of	143
centre of mental significance	170

F.

	PAGE
Face, zones of	129
expression of, colors tone	216
Failure, the cause of	28
Faith, necessity of	28
three degrees of	225
Feather movement	96
Flexibility	11
Foot	46
Force, law of	168
Form, law of	171
Formula, a universal	174

G.

Gamut of expression in pantomime	177
Genius, definition of	17
Gentleman, attitude of the	68
Gentlemen, position of, in introduction to ladies	67
Gerome	7
Gesture, the language of emotion or soul	36
the interpreter of sentiment	38
from significant zones	49
forms of expression for	65
external and interior	60, 118
duration of retaining a	118
inflections of	124
effect of passion on	168
effect of thought on	168
effect of love on	168
precedes speech	170
rhythm of	171
Gladiator oppositions	102
Glottis, "direct attack" of	189
God, as represented by the ancients	32
Godhead, the	33
Groan	195
Guilmette, Dr.	108
Guttmann's "Gymnastics of the Voice"	188

INDEX. 263

H.

	PAGE.
Hand	89, 99
faces of	89
functions of	89
description of movement	90
indications of	91
conditional attitudes of	92
chart of	97
relative attitudes of	99
positions of, in space relative to the centres of gravity and being	99
attitudes of, color the voice	95, 216
inflections of	100
affirmations of	103
Hard work required	12, 27, 28, 78
Harmonic poise of bearing	17
Harmony	171
Haydn, anecdote of	227
Head	42, 43
zones of	41, 129
sympathy with strong leg	18, 71
chart of zones of	131
attitudes of	132
inflections of	134
chart of attitudes of	135
chart of divisions of	136
active divisions of	137
Heart, the, metaphor for love	44
Heraldry	221
High notes for tender sentiments	208
Hip	49
How to move others	190
Hypnotic experiments	62

I.

Idea, main	196
Imagination	78
Imitation, insufficiency of	40, 78
Indulgences, continued, result of	65

	PAGE
Inflection	193
the language of the sensitive nature	36
in gesture	193
pantomime to the blind	193
particular	195
principles of	196
should harmonize	207
Insanity, the gaze of	140
Inspiration, trusting to	5
Intensity of effect, how to produce	189
Interior sensations, caused by outer manifestations and attitudes,	63
memory	64
Interjection	194, 205
Intonation, caressing	208
Introduction	3
Involution	174
Iris	220
Isis	32, 221

J.

Jasper	225
Jaw	161
Jupiter	32

K.

"Key of the universe"	37
Knee	49
Knight's shield, colors of	221
Koran, quotation from	223

L.

Lamentation	195
Language, vocal, dynamic, buccal	36
Larynx	189, 201
heart in the	190
Laugh	196
Legs	46, 57, 66
sections of	41
attitudes of	66

INDEX. 265

	PAGE
Legs illustrated by photographed statues: A faun, Hebe, youth in Parthenon frieze, Pallas Athene, Ariadne, Demosthenes, Diana, Modesty, fighting gladiator	71
chart of	72
Ligure	225
Limbs, 42, (legs and arms)	66
progression of articulations of	173
Lips	161
Little finger, expressive of the affections	92
Louvre, the museum of	20, 40, 62
Lungs	189
are mental	44

M.

Macbeth, a scene from	216
Mackaye, Steele	7
Madelène, Laure de la, quotation from	211
Madeley, quotation from	223
Man the object of art	36
spirit of, imprisoned	40
three types in	64
communicates in three ways	197
Martellato	189
Matter has no form of itself	34
Melody	171
Mental vision	231
Method, proper use of	229
Michael Angelo	231
Mill	5
Milton, quotation from	220
Mind and heart, necessity of culture of	40
Mirror, use of a	11, 25
Mithas	32
Mixed or heart-voice, how to acquire	190
Monad principle	32
Monotone	193, 196
Monroe, Lewis B.	8, 37, 196
Monsabre	5

	PAGE.
Moral division	119
poise	20
Motion, law of	168
and emotion	171
Mouth, expressions of	161
chart of	164
Movement, simultaneous and successive	173
Music, degrees for	211
Mythene	32

N.

Nanterre	3
Natural intuition	17
Negation, fact of	197
Nervous control, value of	22
Ninefold accord	32
chart of	39
Normal form, curves of	18
motion, definition of	37
Nose, Roman, Greek, Turk's	43
expressions of	156
chart of	159
Notes, progressive value of	213
Number three, the, held sacred	32

O.

Ontology, definition of	58
Onyx	225
Opposition, lines of	20
law of	24, 172
Order of exercises for systematic practice	236
Organism, analyzation of	36
Oromazes	32
Orus	32
Osiris	32, 221

P.

Pallas Athene	32
Pantomime, grammar of	167
a gamut of expression in	177

	PAGE
Pantomime, its relation to speech	170
inflection to the deaf	193
Participle	204
Parting advice	227
Pasca	5
Passion	209
tendency of	169
influenced by color	225
People, vulgar and uncultured	209
Pharynx	189
Phrase, Delsarte's method of differentiating	194
modifying	197
rising	211
dissonant note in	212
Physiognomy and phrenology	44
Physiology, definition of	58
Plato, quotation from	77
Platonic hypothesis	33
Portal, quotation from	223
Preposition	205
Previous lessons, how to use	227
Primary oppositions of arm and head	117
Profiles	155
chart of	155
Progressions, ascending	209
Promethean spark, the	40
Pronoun	205
Pythagoras	32

R.

Rachel	5, 79
Rainbow, used in illustration	31, 221
Reäction, law of	172
Registers	190
Regnier, M.	3, 6, 63
Respiration	187
Respiratory and vocal organs, correct use of	188
Rhythm	171

268   INDEX.

	PAGE.
Run, the	82
of women	82
Ruskin	5, 214, 232
quotations from 28, 60, 77, 78, 221, 228, 230	

S.

Sampson, M., quotations from 7,	46
interpreter for Rachel	79
Sapphire	224
Sardius	224
Scholar, attitude of the	68
Selections, directions for analyzing and practicing	216
Semeiotics, definition of	57
science of 61,	64
Sentiment	209
Sequence, law of	170
Serapis, oracle of	32
Serpentine movement	96
Shade, vocal 193, 194, 208,	210
Shoulder 107,	173
as a thermometer 42,	47
Sigh	195
Signs, musical	214
Silence, father of a word	203
Singing	196
Sinuousness, how to acquire	23
Slide	197
Sob	195
Sontag	5
Spencer	5
Spiral movement	108
Spirit, definition of	60
Spiritual love, three degrees of	225
St. Augustine, quotation from	64
St. Genevieve, church of	3
St. Paul, quotation from	34
St. Pierre, quotation from	225
Stones, arrangement and signification of	224
Strength, conscious	168

INDEX.   269

	PAGE.
Stuart, William	8
Study, meaning of	27
and toil	78
reason for	229
Substantive	204
Swedenborg, quotations from	33, 34
System, basis of the	29

T.

Talma	79
Teaching, false system of	231
Technique, attention to	28
Temperament, trusting to	6
Thermometers of passion	169
Thigh, movement of	75
strength of	74
its part in walking	46, 74
Thinker, attitude of the	68
Thought, tendency of	169
Three, the vital number	37
things to be borne in mind	85
Thumb	173
as a thermometer	92
significance of the attitudes of	93, 94
Thummim, stones in	223
Titian	231
Tone, quality of	190
points of reverberation of	191
color of	192
preparation for	196
Topaz	224
Torso	42, 44, 121
zones of	41, 121
attitudes of	122
carriage and expression of	122
inflections of	123
Trial, the Druidical	32
Tribute to Delsarte and Ruskin	232

270 INDEX.

	PAGE.
Trines	224
Trinities of the Hindoos, Egyptians and Chinese	32
Trinity	219
principle of	31
in color	31, 220
requisites of	35, 174
law of	174
Turn, the	82
Types, the, in man	64

U.

Understanding, external	225
Urim, stones in	223

V.

Velocity, law of	171
Venus of Milo	40
Verb	204
"Vere de Vere," caste of	40
Veronese, Paul	229
Vital division	55
Vocal proportions, law of	210
Voice	187
the language of the sensitive nature	36
colored by gesture	95, 192
a caressing hand	190
two kinds of loud	190
quality of, in emotion	192
mental	192
in monotone	193
of the mother	207
strengthened by passion	209
softened by affection	210
Voice-production	189
Vowel, mother	190
excentric, normal, concentric	191
directions for practice	191, 201
normal emission of	192

Vowel, chart of...	199
English, according to Bell...............................	199

W.

Waist-muscles, importance of control of......................	23
Walk, indicative of character................................	73
the perfect..	74
how to...	75
directions for practicing the............................	76
of an actress..	80
of prostration...	81
of dudes...	81
of infancy and inferiority...............................	81
of meditation..	81
of the blind...	81
of the intoxicated.......................................	82
Walking-lesson..	73
Weakness, conscious...	168
Will or desire revealed by the nose..........................	43
Wisdom, internal..	225
Wrist...108,	173
as a thermometer......................................42,	49

www.ingramcontent.com/pod-product-compliance
Lightning Source LLC
Chambersburg PA
CBHW022056230426
43672CB00008B/1189